VALUES,
PROSPERITY,
AND THE
TALMUD

VALUES, PROSPERITY, AND THE TALMUD

BUSINESS LESSONS FROM THE ANCIENT RABBIS

Larry Kahaner

WILEY

John Wiley & Sons, Inc.

This book is dedicated to the memories of my father, Max, and my father-in-law, Bob. I learned from both of their styles.

The first question a person is asked at Judgment after death is "did you deal in good faith in your business?"

—RABA, IN THE TALMUD

One who wishes to acquire wisdom should study the way money works, for there is no greater area of Torah study than this. It is like an overflowing stream.

—RABBI ISHMAEL, IN THE TALMUD

If the statistics are right, the Jews constitute but one percent of the human race. It suggests a nebulous dim puff of star dust lost in the blaze of the Milky Way. Properly, the Jew ought hardly to be heard of; but he is heard of, has always been heard of. He is as prominent on the planet as any other people, and his commercial importance is extravagantly out of proportion to the smallness of his bulk.... All things are mortal but the Jew; all other nations pass, but he remains. What is the secret of his immortality?"

—MARK TWAIN, *AN ESSAY CONCERNING THE JEWS*

CONTENTS

What Can I Learn
about Business from
a 1,500-Year-Old Book?

During the height of their $10 billion empire in the mid-1980s, the Reichmann family's Olympia & York Development, Ltd., was the largest real estate company in North America. This Jewish orthodox family, immigrants to Canada from Hungary, had built a reputation based on integrity, honesty, and on-time delivery of projects, while adhering to their core values of charity and generosity.

When competitors discovered that Paul Reichmann and his brothers studied the Talmud daily, they also began reading it to see if they could glean some of the family's business secrets from this esoteric document. To their dismay, there were no hidden secrets. The Reichmann's business acumen stemmed from the Talmud's practical advice, moral guidance, and ethical values—teachings that the family precisely followed.

The Talmud is one of the cornerstones of Judaism and Jewish culture, but it is not a religious work. The Babylonian Talmud (there is a shorter and somewhat different Palestinian or Jerusalem Talmud) contains about 2½ million words and is composed of discussions and debate among ancient rabbis (*rabbi* means "teacher") that cover virtually every aspect of life, from medicine to child rearing and from business to building a house. Many people consider these volumes a manual for life.

Around the time of the Second Temple in Israel, from 539 to 332 B.C.E. (before the common era) members of the Great Assembly, a group of priests and prominent citizens, began collecting and organizing all the written texts. They decided on their order as well as what works would be included in the Five Books of Moses, or Torah. The Torah, usually seen in the form of parchment scrolls, contains early biblical stories with which most of us are familiar. These scholars also organized another body of text called the Prophets and writings such as Psalms, Proverbs, and Chronicles. These works together constitute the Old Testament, which is part of Hebrew or Jewish Scripture. Jewish Scripture is the foundation of the Old Testament in the Christian Bible and other religious works that followed.

Once completed, these scholars turned their attention to organizing the centuries-old oral works, a hodgepodge of laws, opinions, and stories that had grown unwieldy over the years. These mainly were the Mishnah, oral commentaries on the Torah, and the Gemara, which is commentary on the Mishnah. (The word *Gemara* is sometimes used to mean the Babylonian Talmud and consists of the Mishnah plus commentary on the Mishnah.) When these oral commentaries were finally organized and written down, they formed the Talmud. (For more detail on the formation of the Talmud see "A Short History of the Talmud" in the back of this book.) The charts that follow show how these ancient works fit together.

Although the Talmud is fixed in time, contemporary rabbis still answer questions based on discussions and arguments of the ancient Talmudic rabbis. (For more about these rabbis, check "A Who's Who of Talmudic Rabbis" in the back of this book.)

The Talmud was designed to stimulate conversation and debate through free association and spirited arguments among sages, each

The Jewish or Hebrew Scripture is composed of:

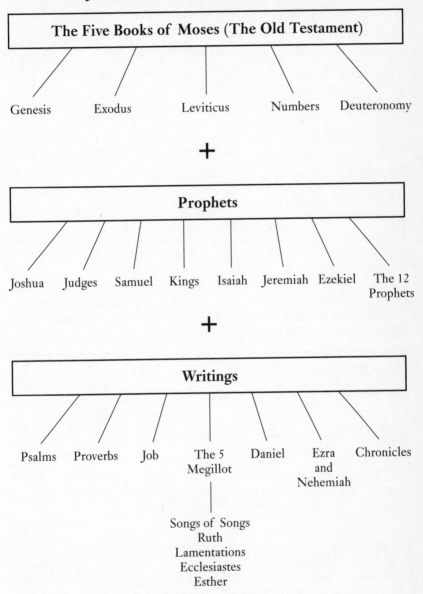

The Five Books of Moses (The Old Testament)

Genesis   Exodus   Leviticus   Numbers   Deuteronomy

+

Prophets

Joshua   Judges   Samuel   Kings   Isaiah   Jeremiah   Ezekiel   The 12 Prophets

+

Writings

Psalms   Proverbs   Job   The 5 Megillot   Daniel   Ezra and Nehemiah   Chronicles

Songs of Songs
Ruth
Lamentations
Ecclesiastes
Esther

*Note: Some scholars use the term *Torah* to refer to the five books of Moses; some use it to refer to the entire Jewish Scripture.

The Talmud is composed of:

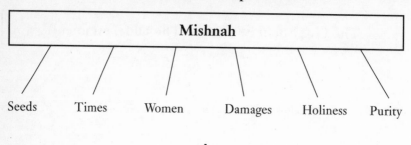

Mishnah

Seeds   Times   Women   Damages   Holiness   Purity

+

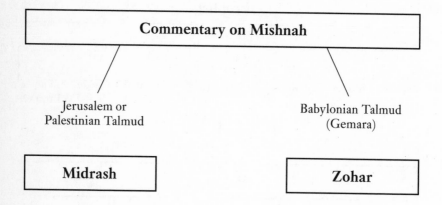

Commentary on Mishnah

Jerusalem or
Palestinian Talmud

Babylonian Talmud
(Gemara)

Midrash		Zohar

+

Post-Talmudic Works

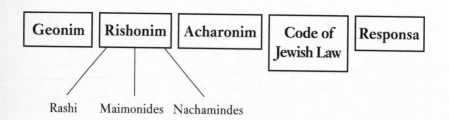

Geonim	Rishonim	Acharonim	Code of Jewish Law	Responsa

Rashi   Maimonides   Nachamindes

The Christian Bible is composed of:

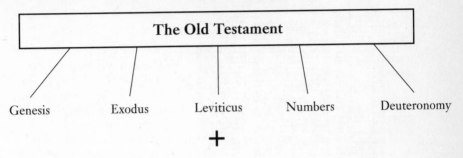

The Old Testament

Genesis   Exodus   Leviticus   Numbers   Deuteronomy

+

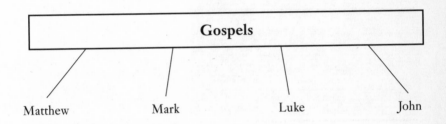

Gospels

Matthew   Mark   Luke   John

+

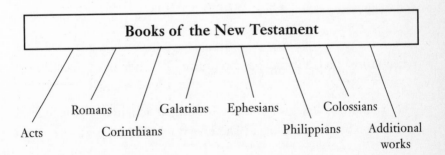

Books of the New Testament

Acts   Romans   Corinthians   Galatians   Ephesians   Philippians   Colossians   Additional works

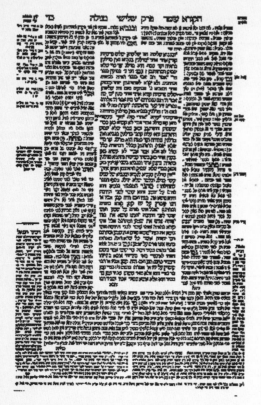

This is a typical page of Talmud. The text in the middle is the Mishnah or commentary. The text surrounding the Mishnah explains, comments, and expands on individual words or phrases found in the Mishnah. An explanation can continue for many pages. *(Thanks to Eliezer Segal for this contribution.)*

setting forth his own beliefs. Ideas and discussions go off on tangents, come back, and loop around themselves. There are no large sections on business or medicine, however. Specific topics can be found in clusters, but more often than not they are scattered throughout the book. While this nonlinear structure makes the Talmud tough to grasp, it also lends it richness. Readers are forced to stop, think, ask questions, and deliberate.

Why the Emphasis on Business?

The Talmud covers a wide range of human activities, but it focuses intently on business dealings. (The Five Books of Moses alone contain

613 direct commandments, and more than 100 concern business and economics.) The Talmudic sage Raba said that when a person dies, the first question he or she will be asked in heaven is "Did you deal honestly in business?"[1] And Rabbi Ishmael stated, "One who wishes to acquire wisdom should study the way money works, for there is no greater area of Torah study than this. It is like an ever flowing stream..."[2]

Why this interest in business and, by extension, money and profit? This emphasis certainly seems to solidify the stereotype of Jews as being overly concerned with money. However, that superficial view is far from the true nature of Judaism and what the Talmudic rabbis were trying to convey.

Here are the main reasons that the Talmudic rabbis spent a lot of time discussing business, commerce, and money:

- The Talmud stresses the importance of dealing honestly in business because transacting business, more than any other human activity, tests our moral mettle and reveals our character.

- Working, money, and commerce offer us some of the best opportunities to do good deeds such as giving charity, providing employment, and building prosperity for our communities and the world.

It is through money and commerce that we reveal our human frailties, our bigotry, and our ability to deal justly with others when our natural instinct is to maximize our profits no matter what the consequences. We are sometimes tempted to cheat in business transactions because we think that everyone's doing it or that big companies won't be injured by our minuscule transgressions or that we'll never again have to encounter the other party to the transaction. In the Talmud, no transaction is tiny and no transgression is trivial.

The Talmudic rabbis laid down specific guidelines for running businesses, handling workers, buying and selling goods, forming partnerships, making agreements, paying taxes, and even advertising products.

While ethical business practices should be a reward unto themselves, the Talmud also demonstrates that operating a business in an ethical manner is good for a company's bottom line and for the community at large.

As you read through the Talmud's business lessons, you will see overarching ethical themes emerge. These values form the basis of Talmudic thought, which, of course, stems from Jewish ethical beliefs. Some of these ideas were incorporated into other religions—Christianity and Islam, for example—but most of the ideas remain uniquely Talmudic, and are summarized as follows:

1. *The Golden Rule rules.*

    The Talmudic rabbis discussed people's relationship to God, but they were often more interested in the relationships among people—how we treat each other. The Golden Rule—"Love thy neighbor as thyself"—is the basic guideline for these relationships. When challenged by a heathen scoffer to teach him the Torah in its simplest form, Rabbi Hillel remarked, "Whatever is hateful unto thee, do it not to thy fellow man. This is the whole of Torah. The rest is commentary."

2. *There is no such thing as absolute ownership.*

    We are stewards. God owns everything in the universe, and we are the caretakers. This responsibility applies to the earth itself, as well as other people, animals, money, and businesses—in short, everything. We are bound to protect these resources and use them wisely. We are not to waste any resources, natural or artificial, because they are not ours to dispose of.

3. *We are responsible for any damage that we cause.*

    The biblical phrase "an eye for an eye" does not have anything to do with punishment for knocking out someone's eye, and it is not an endorsement of the death penalty. It means that we are responsible for everything that we do. If we break something, we are expected to fix it, replace it, pay for it, or otherwise make restitution.

The corollary is that we are also obligated to prevent damage to or the destruction of anything unnecessarily. This includes anything that happens as a result of our action or our *inaction*. This prohibition refers not only to material things but to intangibles such as another person's self-esteem or reputation.

4. *Show compassion for those weaker than ourselves.*

This tenet requires that we offer charity to those poorer than ourselves. It also means that we should not take advantage of those less fortunate than ourselves in daily business matters. Jewish Scripture says it this way: "Don't place a stumbling block before the blind." This also means that you don't sell a dangerous weapon to a mentally ill person and you don't sell alcohol to a minor, because they're not capable of handling these things.

5. *We all have free will.*

"Everything is foreseen, yet freedom of choice is given." This fundamental aphorism from the Talmud seems at cross-purposes, but it is not. Although God knows the future, we are all responsible for making our own choices, since we don't know what God's plan is.

Although we may not be able to control what others do to us, we are fully in charge of our own behavior and actions. Whether we succeed or fail, whether we behave properly or improperly, is up to us.

6. *The law of the land is the law.*

The Talmudic rabbis believed that society can force moral behavior upon its citizens. Everyone in the community is obligated to follow the majority's law. This means we must pay our taxes, abide by court rulings, and follow local customs pertaining to business and commerce.

7. *Enough is enough.*

The Talmud stresses balance in all aspects of life. Being rich can be wonderful, but too much wealth brings its own burdens. On the extreme opposite side, poverty is one of the worst fates to befall a person. Work is vital, but working too much is bad for you. The rabbis believed that by living a balanced existence, you will enjoy a fulfilled and joyous life.

A Handbook for Today's Business World

As modern business life becomes increasingly complicated and difficult, managers are turning to the classics for guidance. Sun Tzu's *The Art of War* has become a handbook for how to handle market competitors. Machiavelli's *The Prince*, now standard reading in business schools, has enjoyed a resurgence in popularity because of its clarity and vision, despite its ruthless approach.

The Talmudic view is often not what you would expect. For example, the Talmudic rabbis view money and profit not as sources of evil, as in some religions, but as opportunities to do good works, in general raising people's standard of living so they can spend more time with their families, study important works of wisdom, and enjoy life's pleasures. On the other hand, money poses us some of life's greatest challenges—such as overcoming greed and knowing when enough is enough.

The Talmud offers riches to anyone brave enough to explore its depths. A beacon for the Jews, the Talmud has survived censorship and wholesale burnings. Its adherents have been tortured and murdered for studying it. Against all odds, both the Talmud and the Jews have survived, each enriching the other. The Talmud has endured because its message is vital and its wisdom is ageless.

This book serves as a guide to the Talmud's business wisdom. It will teach you how to run a successful business, negotiate with style, earn the loyalty of your employees, sell products successfully, advertise effectively, and make higher profits, all within a time-tested ethical and moral framework. These centuries-old subjects are relevant today because human nature has not changed, nor have the fundamentals of business and commerce. Interestingly, the Talmud was codified during a period when the ancient Hebrews lived in an agrarian economy but were moving toward becoming a merchant class. The Talmud reflects the time when these ancient people were figuring out the rules of trade and business.

The lessons of the Talmudic rabbis that appear in this book start with basic but profound ideas about money and work, and then move on to more complicated business issues such as employer-employee relationships, partnerships, and competition.

This book will introduce you to people who use the Talmud's lessons in running their companies. Like Malden Mills owner Aaron Feuerstein, who continued to pay his employees despite having to temporarily close his operation due to a devastating fire, these people study the Talmud and apply its teachings. As Victor Jacobs, chief executive of the successful Allou Health & Beauty Care, in Brooklyn, New York, replied when asked by *Fortune* magazine how studying the Talmud has helped his business, "It opens your mind and teaches you how to think."

The Talmud's Greatest Gift

As you read, you'll begin to understand the Talmud's most important gift to modern businesspeople—something that we all strive for but few of us reach.

The Talmud offers a way to happily blend our business, personal, and spiritual lives—and be successful at each of them. It offers precise instructions for balancing the need for business success with the need for a satisfying life outside of work. The Talmud accomplishes this by challenging readers to think in new and different ways about their jobs, their attitudes toward money, and their notions of the purpose of commerce. The Talmud confronts students with fundamental questions such as "Why do we work?," "Why do businesses exist?," and "How much money should we make?" The rabbis' answers to these questions may seem strange, they may even shock, but they will challenge you to discover your own ideas.

No matter what your religious beliefs—even if you have no religious convictions at all—the Talmud's ideas will forever change the way you think about yourself, your business, and your family—for the better.

NUMBERED REFERENCES

[1]Sabbath, 31a
[2]Bava Batra, 175b

ACKNOWLEDGMENTS

I want to thank many people for help in researching and writing this book. Some spent a great deal of their time, sharing their wisdom with me, while others helped me over some rough spots by offering a new idea or approach that directed me to the best path.

I am grateful for assistance from Cop Macdonald, a long-time friend and purveyor of wisdom; Martin Rutte, coauthor of *Chicken Soup for the Soul at Work* (Health Communications, 2001), whose encouragement played a crucial role; Doug Starr, whose instincts were on target; Alan Green, a friend and former coauthor, who encouraged me from the beginning; Bob Meyers, president of the National Press Foundation and former colleague, who offered his experience on the importance of a day of rest; Paul Bateman, of the Silver Institute, whose global business ideas were inspiring; Joel Makower, author and friend, who helped me understand the interconnection between business and the environment.

A special thanks to those in my writer's group, which has been meeting every month for over 12 years: Alan Appel, Audie Appel, Dan Stashower, John McKeon, and Marc Smolonsky—all accomplished authors in their own right; Reb Zalman M. Schachter-Shalomi, professor of religious studies and director of the Center for Engaged Spirituality at Naropa University and professor emeritus of religion, Temple University; Rabbi Nahum Ward-Lev, former rabbi of Santa Fe's Temple Beth Shalom and coordinator of Ghost Ranch's Spirituality at Work Project; Rabbi Mordechai Liebling, Torah of Money director, The Shefa Fund; Rabbi Meir Tamari, former chief economist, Office of the Governor of the Bank of Israel in Jerusalem and founder of the Center for Business Ethics, who spent time with me despite his busy schedule; long-time friend Steve McMenamin, executive director of the Greenwich Roundtable, for his insights into financial markets; Jeff Danko of the Shefa Fund; Professor Hersh Friedman, deputy chair of business at Brooklyn College, whose articles and phone conversations helped me get started on my research; Eliezer Segal, professor of religious studies, University of Calgary; Ohr Somayach, whose online "ask the rabbi" service promptly answered questions; my editor Airié Stuart and assistant Emily Conway for their guidance, enthusiasm, and insight; and my agent Gail Ross, whom I got to know again after a too-long hiatus.

The Spirituality of Money

Who is wealthy? One who derives inner peace from his fortune.
—RABBI MEIR[1]

Some religions reject the love of money, contending that it is the root of all evil. Some go so far as to say that poverty is a route to holiness and scarcity is a road to sanctity. The Talmudic rabbis' attitude, in contrast, is that money and wealth can be positive forces.

Two conditions must be met for money to be a positive force, however. First, we must use our wealth in a responsible way, and, second, we must understand that wealth is not an indication of our inner worth. We are merely stewards of the wealth bestowed upon us while we are alive.

Praying for Prosperity

In ancient times, at the conclusion of Yom Kippur, the holiest day of the year, the high priest blessed the congregation. His prayer was for enough rain so the fields would yield a robust crop. He prayed that the congregation would reap a large harvest, beyond what they would need to feed themselves, so they could sell the surplus crops in the marketplace and prosper financially.

The later Talmudic rabbis were somewhat troubled by the high priest's approach. Why would he pray for financial prosperity instead of, say, health, happiness, wisdom, or some other nonmaterialistic, spiritual desire?

The high priest certainly wanted people to think about God and their spirituality, but he knew that unless people had money, they could not even begin to think about their spiritual health. If people were not able to attain some measure of material comfort, their spiritual needs would never be addressed.

Rabbi Elazar ben Azaryah said, "Where there is no money, there is no learning."[2] This is the literal translation, but the rabbis expanded it to mean that unless people's stomachs are full, they cannot study, grow spiritually, and do good deeds. The ultimate purpose of money, which we'll see time and again in Talmudic thought, is to increase community prosperity, provide employment, and allow people to grow and reach their full potential.

There Is No Virtue in Poverty

The Talmudic rabbis recognized no virtue in poverty—intentional or otherwise. They found nothing noble in people's becoming impoverished by giving away their money, no matter how worthy the cause. By Halakic law (Halakah are Talmudic passages concerning law and legal subjects), Jews are forbidden to give away their fortunes and become poor. Contrast this with Matthew 19:21 in the King James Version of the Christian Bible, which tells people, "Sell what you have and give to the poor." This is not to suggest that the Gospel of Matthew is wrong or misguided, but it shows that Judaism takes a different approach than many other religions. Some Buddhists, for example, believe that a true connection to the spiritual realm comes as a result of a paucity of possessions.

Interestingly, the ancient rabbis often suggested that rich people obviously were more righteous than others because they had been blessed with wealth. Naturally, this observation didn't always hold true because a wealthy person's righteousness depended on how he spent his money—on whether he did good deeds with it. Nonetheless, in ancient times rich people were often revered in Jewish communities not because of their wealth, per se, but because they were thought to be blessed, until shown to be otherwise.

Judaism considers donating one-twentieth to one-tenth of your wealth virtuous, but giving more of your estate is considered excessive unless you are very wealthy (although it's acceptable to bequeath an entire estate prior to your death). Taking care of your own needs and those of your family takes priority.

The story of Job is a classic Bible tale about a righteous, God-fearing, wealthy man, and it reveals the horrors of being poor. The story suggests that Job was wealthy because he was a good person and thus was rewarded by God. Satan challenges God, asking whether Job would still praise him if he were poor and had life-threatening diseases. God takes the challenge and turns Job's life upside down, giving him boils and sores and thrusting him into poverty. Job's wife and others tell him to renounce God, but Job refuses, despite his afflictions.

In the end, Job becomes twice as wealthy as he had been, but during an interchange we hear Job discussing how important money is to him. God asks Job, "Which would you prefer, poverty or afflictions?" Job responds, "I would rather accept all the afflictions of the world, but not poverty." It's interesting to see that, faced with physical ills and even death, Job would prefer these choices over poverty because he understood that without some amount of money, his life and the lives of his family members would be miserable.

A POOR MAN'S LIFE IS NOT A LIFE

One of the most intriguing comments about poverty is the following: "A poor man's life is not a life."[1] Although it seems to say, somewhat cruelly, that a poor person's life isn't complete and, by implication, that a rich person's life is superior, the intention is not malicious at all.

A poor person does not have the same opportunities to do good deeds, so his life is not as blessed as that of a rich person who can do good things with his wealth. However, this is not to say that a poor person can't do good deeds. In fact, even poor people are expected to use their money to help others. Unfortunately, the reality is that poor people are often reluctant to perform acts of charity because they have so little money.

[1]Bezah, 32b

The Talmudic rabbis had a great personal interest in discussing poverty because so many of them were relatively poor. Passages from the Talmud frequently reflect this, for example: "A poor man's life is no life," "Poverty deprives a man of his creator," and "A poor man is like one dead." Another passage states: "Nothing in the universe is worse than poverty. It is the most terrible of sufferings. A person oppressed by poverty is like someone who carries on his shoulders the weight of the world's sufferings. If all the pain and all the suffering of this world were placed on one side of the scale and poverty on the other, the balance would tilt toward poverty."[3]

The Talmudic rabbis examined not only how poverty caused people to lose sight of their creator and their spiritual side, but also how it can undermine self-esteem and self-confidence, both of which are necessary for personal and business success. Rabbi Yohannan and Rabbi Eleazer said that as soon as a man became dependent on others for his sustenance, his face would change as many colors as a *kerum*.

The *kerum,* an African bird, changes hue depending on how the sun hits it. In analogous fashion, a poverty-stricken man is buffeted by events around him, eventually losing control of his life, his family, and his career.

I'VE GOT GOOD NEWS AND BAD NEWS

Being poor brings on obvious problems, including family discord. "When the barley is gone from the jar, strife comes knocking at the door."[1] We know from contemporary studies that the number one subject that married couples argue about is money—mainly, the lack of it.

But having lots of money has its drawbacks, too. Money challenges us to use our wealth responsibly and wisely, a talent that some of us may not possess. One of the responsibilities of wealth is to learn what to do with money and not be a cheapskate. The rabbis note, "Where there is wealth, there should be no penny-pinching."[2]

[1]Bava Metzia, 59a
[2]Sabbath, 102b

Is It Good to Be Wealthy?

If poverty is to be avoided, is wealth to be sought? This issue was thornier for the Talmudic rabbis. Although being rich was considered better than being poor, being wealthy entails many challenges, including greater obligations and loftier responsibilities. "The more possessions, the more anxiety," Hillel noted.[4]

First, it's essential to understand how Judaism regards ownership. Judaism provides for a right to property and protection for that property, but it does not accept the idea of absolute and unlimited ownership. Wealth, consisting of both money and property, does not belong to the individual; it belongs to God. People are stewards, or trustees, of that wealth.

LOVE GOD WITH ALL OF OUR MONEY?

"One should love God with all one's heart, all one's life and all one's money."[1]

In this Talmudic passage, the rabbis say that we should love God with all of our money in addition to loving him with our hearts and lives. Why is it necessary to spell this out when we already pledge our lives to the Almighty?

The purpose of this passage is to help us reach people who regard money as more important than their lives. We all know people (and the ancient rabbis did, too) whose jobs and money come before their own lives and those of their family members. Many of us have friends or relatives who have suffered heart attacks or other diseases to which overwork, worry, and stress were contributing factors. Yet these people continue to work long hours in jobs that caused them illness. Because money is so important to these people, they should follow the rabbis' advice and elevate their love of money to the same status as their love of God, which means that they should thereby love God enough to follow his commandment to slow down and live a more balanced life.

[1]Berachot, 54a

Rabbi Akiva regarded wealth as a long-term debt to God, which is paid off by living a righteous life. He said, "Everything is given as a pledge, and a net is spread for all the living. The shop is open and the shopkeeper extends credit. The ledger is open and the hand writes. Whoever wishes to borrow may come and borrow. The collectors make their appointed rounds daily and take payment from man, whether he knows it or not. The judgment is the judgment of truth and everything is prepared for the banquet."[5] In this passage, God is the shopkeeper who has loaned us money, our businesses, our lives—everything. In return, the debtor owes the Almighty a righteous life. Our days on earth are limited, and we are expected to settle our accounts before we die. The payment should not come at the last minute, either, but through a life of good deeds.

In this vein, wealthy people are expected to act as trustees for their riches and use this wealth to alleviate suffering. This does not mean that wealth should be redistributed so that all people become financially equal. On the contrary, we must accept that there will always be both rich and poor in the world. For the rabbis, this inevitable fact of life makes charity imperative.

There's an Chasidic story about a wealthy businessman who decided to retire. (Chasids, a sect of Jewish mystics established in Poland about 1750, are characterized by religious zeal and a spirit of prayer, joy, and charity.) He wanted to close his factory, which was operating profitably, and spend the rest of his life studying the Talmud. He told the local rabbi about his plans, and he expected the rabbi to applaud his choice to become a man of great Talmudic wisdom. Instead, the rabbi was dismayed at the man's decision and asked, "What will happen to all the workers you employ? How will they feed their families?" The rabbi explained to the factory owner that perhaps God gave him this wealth so that he would act as its trustee, and thus he had a moral obligation to use it properly for the benefit of those in his community. His job was to provide jobs.

Judaism proposes that, although wealth is a good and positive condition, it cannot, in itself, bring happiness. The insatiable quest for wealth that is evident all around us can become self-defeating and destructive for those who become caught up in it.

In *The Challenge of Wealth*, the contemporary rabbi Meir Tamari describes this challenge as the ability to understand that enough is enough. The concept of "enough is enough" runs throughout Talmudic thought and is crucial to the lesson that discusses overwork. People must resist their natural inclination to accumulate more wealth than they need because this increases the temptation to acquire money though dishonest activities. Tamari explains, "Greed is enhanced and empowered by man's perpetual fear of economic uncertainty. So we perpetually seek to protect ourselves against the risk involved in the market and in the human condition through legitimate means but also by immoral ones." He adds that if people have faith that God will provide them sustenance, then they will be released from the desire to seek more money and property than they really need: "...it is this faith that allows people to take the risks needed for entrepreneurial development, thus maintaining the legitimate search for wealth within moral parameters."

MONEY, FAITH, AND THE FUTURE

The Talmudic rabbis had great faith that God's abundance would be given to those who worked for it. This faith *should* reduce the anxiety and worry about what would happen in the future. Rabbi Eliezer the Elder said, "He who has a loaf of bread in his basket but says, 'What will I eat tomorrow?' is lacking in faith."[1]

Rabbi Simeon ben Eleazer noted that worrying about tomorrow is a useless occupation. "Attend to what comes to hand, what you have the means for and what is still within your power. If you defer today's needs and its obligations until tomorrow, then tomorrow will have more than enough to cope with its own needs. How can it handle those of yesterday?"[2]

A more sobering and severely practical look at the future came from Ben Sira, who remarked, "Do not be distressed about tomorrow's troubles because you do not know what tomorrow will bring. When tomorrow comes, you may be dead and you would have worried about a world that is not yours."[3]

[1]Sotah, 48b
[2]Sabbath, 151b
[3]Yevamot, 63b

Tamari's point is an important one because it forges the direct link between spirituality and money that many of us seek.

Having faith in God's blessing of continual abundance frees people from the belief that they must accumulate too much wealth or that they must do so through immoral activity. If we *truly* believe that God offers us abundance, then there is no need to steal or cheat to attain what we want. There will be enough for us. On the other hand, if we believe that the "big pie" is shrinking, then we will feel impelled to get our slice quickly by whatever means necessary so we are not left out. Clearly, this latter road can lead to illegal behavior and ultimate ruin.

> *Having faith in God's blessing of continual abundance frees people from the belief that they must accumulate too much wealth or that they must do so through immoral activity.*

We also must be certain that others do not suffer, either directly or indirectly, because of our wealth. In his book *The Kabbalah of Money*, Rabbi Nilton Bonder defines wealth in a unique way: "Let us define wealth as the highest form of organization possible to the environment in such a way that everything alive and everything essential to life exists without scarcity. In other words, the more abundance we create for a given human need, without generating the scarcity of another need, the better."

This definition reveals a connection between spirituality and money that many of us have never considered because we often think of money as the antithesis of spirituality. We tend to regard money as being rooted in earthly matters, while spirituality exists on a higher plane. However, this positive, spiritual view of money is validated when the money is used to perform good deeds on earth and nobody is hurt as a consequence of the quest for great wealth. If these and other criteria are met, the seeking of wealth becomes a noble and divine pursuit.

THE TALMUD ON INVESTING

No discussion of money is complete without discussing investing. Although the ancient rabbis may not have envisioned our modern, robust stock markets, they had their own sophisticated commodities futures markets in crops, and they invested in partnerships and land purchases.

The two best investing tips that can be gleaned from the ancient rabbis are to engage in value investing and to diversify. In today's markets, most equities investors are one of two types. Value investors buy undervalued stocks and hold them until other investors appreciate their worth and reward the stock price. Growth investors catch a stock's growth wave, keep it until it falls out of favor, and then sell it. During the late-1990s dot-com mania, growth investing was in vogue. In the early 2000s, value investing is in style.

Over the long term, value investing has outperformed growth investing, as demonstrated by Warren Buffett, the world's most famous value investor. The ancient rabbis believed this, too. "When merchandise is held in low esteem, at rock bottom prices, go and buy it up, for in the end its price will rise," Bar Kapara advises.[1]

The rabbis were adamant about diversification. Rabbi Isaac advised, "A man should divide his money into three parts: one third in land, one third in merchandise and one third at hand."[2] Likewise, farmers were advised to divide their land into three parts, planting different crops in each section, to avoid bankruptcy in case one crop failed as a result of pests or adverse weather conditions.

Investors who were diversified and whose portfolios contained value stocks were able to withstand the technology sector crash of 2000 and the lagging market that followed. Unfortunately, many growth stock aficionados and undiversified, tech-heavy investors were wiped out.

[1]Tanhuma, Mispatim, 5
[2]Bava Metzia, 42a

Seeking a Balance

The ancient rabbis suggested that Jews are obligated to study the Torah and the Talmud because this is a time-consuming activity and is therefore time that will *not* be spent accumulating wealth. Thus, studying helps people to achieve an equilibrium between accumulating money and appreciating the other parts of life. Likewise, simply choosing to leave the office at 5 P.M. rather than working late may help people develop more balanced lives by allowing them more time with their families.

KEEP IT MOVING

"Why are the coins called zuzim? Because they circulate from hand to hand."[1]

The Hebrew word *zuzim,* plural form of *zuz,* meaning an ancient coin, is similar to the word *zazim,* which means "hand to hand." (Another interpretation is that coins were named after Zeus, whose likeness appeared on them.) To the rabbis, money is at its best when it's changing hands, circulating to do good deeds for people and businesses, and building prosperity in communities. Money is underutilized, the rabbis believed, when it sits in a vault.

Current monetary policy also holds that the money supply must be robust and liquid for economies to flourish and businesses to grow. It is incumbent upon central banks, like the Federal Reserve in the United States, to make sure money is readily available for loans for business growth.

[1]Bemidar Rabbah, 22, 8

Tamari notes that seeking this balance is difficult, and his views echo those of Rabbi Jonathan Eybeshitz, an eighteenth-century European

Talmudist who considered money one of the greatest trials and temptations of life. This challenge has been particularly trying for Jews, suggested Eybeshitz, because the religion does not preach that money is evil or that worldly pleasures should be totally shunned. In fact, one passage from the Talmud states that Jews will be held accountable for the pleasures in life in which they did not partake, including the visceral pleasures that money can bring.

Concerning the challenge of achieving balance, Eybeshitz wrote: "Our natural needs are important and pleasures are not to be renounced. Man requires material things to live, and Judaism is not calculated to bring pain but joy and happiness to man. Our religion does not require a self-inflicted discipline or self-sacrifice, fasting and flagellation. We are not expected to live as hermits nor a life of self-denial." Judaism advocates "not the total abstention from physical comforts but the judicious use of them."

Delight in One's Lot

Judaism teaches that the truly wealthy people (or companies) are those who appreciate what they have attained. A wealthy person is one who achieves a peaceful state of mind through his money. This implies that a wealthy person has neither a lot of money nor a little money. A billionaire would not be considered wealthy if he was not satisfied with what he had, yet a poor person would be considered wealthy if he was happy with his small lot.

A wealthy person is one who achieves a peaceful state of mind through his money.

AN EYE-OPENING STORY ABOUT GREED

Upon meeting a group of rabbis, Alexander the Great asked them to pay him homage. Referring to the Hebrew God, Alexander said to the rabbis, "I too am a king. I am also of some account; give me something."[1]

They gave him an eyeball, which he placed on a balance scale. He put gold and silver on the other side. No matter how much gold and silver he placed opposite the eyeball, he could not outweigh it. He said to the rabbis, "How can this be?" They replied, "It is the eyeball of a human being, which is never satisfied."

Still not sure that this was true, and thinking that the rabbis were toying with him, Alexander asked the rabbis to prove their argument. They took dust off the table and covered the eyeball so it could not see the precious metals and long for them. Immediately, the scales tipped as the eyeball was outweighed by the gold and silver.

The moral of the story is that humans are innately greedy and are never happy with what they have unless they make a special effort to be satisfied.

[1]Tamid, 32b

The Book of Proverbs says: "Lest I become sated and deny, saying 'who is God?' or lest I become impoverished and steal thus profaning the name of my God."[6] In other words, if we have everything we want materially, we might believe that God has nothing to do with our wealth, that we did it all on our own. That might lead to denying the existence of God altogether. On the other hand, if we were so poor that we stole for sustenance, we would break God's commandments as well. This passage calls for balance in our financial lives.

THE TALMUD AND THE LOTTERY

Wouldn't it be great to win the lottery? According to the Talmudic rabbis, gaining quick wealth through the miracle of picking the right numbers, rather than through hard work and risk taking, might not be a good thing for your spirit.

There is a story of a man whose wife died in childbirth. This father had to feed the infant, but he could not afford a wet nurse. Then a miracle happened: The man sprouted breasts, and he was able to feed his son.

Rabbi Yosef said, "A miracle of nature has happened for this man!" Abaye had the opposite reaction. "This is a sad story," he said. "The orderliness of the universe was changed for this man."[1]

The story demonstrates that those who rely on the consistent nature of the world—orderly financial markets, for example—are truly blessed because the world is in sync with them. They work at being rich, so they are more likely to appreciate what they have attained. Most important, their money comes with responsibilities, such as continuing to build businesses and employ workers—unlike lottery winners, whose money comes with no strings attached and without an ongoing plan for spending the money. It's no surprise, then, that studies of lottery winners have shown that a year after their "miracle," most of them are no happier than nonwinners.

Proverbs 20:21 also contains an admonition about quick wealth: "Wealth obtained by vanity shall be diminished, but he who gathers little by little shall increase." This means that wealth received because you are good-looking or young—what Scripture terms "vanity"—will not last, whereas money obtained by hard work in an incremental fashion will remain with you.

[1]Sabbath, 53b

"Who is rich?" the Talmudic rabbis asked each other. One rabbi replied that it is the man who has a bathroom near his dining room. (In ancient times, having your own personal privy close to the house was a perk of the rich.) Another said that a rich person is one who has a hundred fields, a hundred vineyards, and a hundred slaves in each of them. (The slaves referred to in the Talmud were not slaves as we would define them. Slavery is forbidden by Jewish law. These slaves were actually indentured servants who were working off a debt or other legal obligation and were paid a fair wage for their services.)

Rabbi Meir had the last word in the discussion, saying, "Who is wealthy? One who derives inner peace from his fortune." If your money does not help to bring you a measure of spiritual comfort, then it is worthless.

Money and the Afterlife

If money is a means to an end, meaning it should be used for good deeds, then it is imperative to convert money to good deeds before death. The idea of an afterlife exists in Jewish belief, but it does not play the same prominent role that it does in some other religions. All that will accompany people to the afterlife are their deeds and reputation.

In his book *The Jewish Encyclopedia of Moral and Ethical Issues,* Nachum Amsel recounted the Ashkenazi custom of the Middle Ages that involved building one's coffin from the wood of the dining room table. Jews of that time believed that the way they behaved around their table—the manner in which they invited people to partake of their hospitality and their generosity—could be carried to the next life through the wood in the dinner table. The wood contained the spirit of their good deeds and the love of their friends, family, and neighbors.

Many religions and belief systems incorporate the concept of "dust to dust," meaning that we come into the world with nothing and leave with nothing. In Ecclesiastes Rabbah 5:14, the ancient rabbis told the story of the fox who found a fenced-in vineyard. The fence had a hole through which the fox wanted to enter, but he was too fat. In order to fit through the hole, the fox fasted for three days until he became thin and somewhat frail. In this weakened condition, he squeezed through the hole and gorged himself on the grapes inside. Eating for several days, he grew fat, but when he tried to leave, he couldn't fit back through the hole. Again, he fasted for three days until he could exit the vineyard through the small hole.

Once outside the vineyard, the fox looked back and shouted, "Vineyard, what good are you? Your fruit is sweet but one cannot eat. As one enters, one must come out."

The rabbis noted that this represents the world in which we live. In terms of material wealth, we come in with nothing, and we leave the same way. The only part of us that lives on is the good deeds we leave behind.

A Company's Attitude toward Money Can Determine Its Success

The way companies regard money can make a big difference to their success or failure. Although the ultimate goal of any business should be profit, the most successful companies heed the Talmud's lessons and do not focus on money for money's sake. They think of money as a vehicle for furthering their objectives: the good deeds of research, greater employment, and community and global prosperity.

For example, Starbucks has learned that fostering environmental values pays dividends, and Gerber profits by putting babies first.

Gerber Products is a 75-year-old, well-respected, profitable company that operates in 80 countries and holds nearly 70 percent of the $1 billion U.S. baby product market. Gerber's management has always focused on babies rather than profits. "The key element is that we do what's right for the baby. Everything stems from that notion," CEO Al

STARBUCKS DOES WELL BY DOING GOOD

Starbucks has made environmental protection a core value of its business. By focusing on this particular value, the company's profits subsequently increase.

In 1998, Starbucks' management was concerned that coffee growing was beginning to negatively affect rain forests, so the company established a $200,000 pilot program to help Mexican farmers grow coffee beans under forest canopy, since coffee needs shade to grow properly. Because this had never been done before, the managers were concerned that the beans might not grow at all and, if they did, that the resulting coffee wouldn't taste very good because the soil conditions were different. They were surprised when the beans grown by the Mexican farmers were excellent. This coffee is selling so well in the United States that the company is now offering it overseas. Starbucks hopes to expand this method of growing beans to other countries.

What started out as a way to help preserve the environment, based on the company's environmental mission established in 1992, also turned out to be profitable. Orin Smith, the company's chief executive, told the *New York Times,* "We risked this for the environment benefits, but it now has the potential to be a really profitable product."

Piergallini told me in an interview for my book *Say It and Live It* (Doubleday, 1998). For instance, the Gerber Parents Resource Center is available to parents 24 hours a day, every day. Specialists at the center answer questions and address concerns about infant care and feeding, even if they're not related to Gerber products. The company also maintains one of the world's largest private research facilities dedicated exclusively to infant nutrition.

Financially successful companies are those in which the primary focus is not making money but satisfying customers, treating employees well, and handling a host of other tasks that may not immediately or directly generate revenue. Only by fulfilling nonmoney concerns can long-term profits eventually flow.

Summary—Lesson One

1. The ultimate role of money is to afford individuals and companies the time and resources to learn, grow spiritually, and do good deeds.

2. The truly wealthy people are those who delight in what they have.

3. Profitable companies have an additional responsibility to do good deeds with their money by increasing community prosperity through jobs.

4. Financially successful companies focus on pleasing customers, respecting employees, and producing excellent products and services. Companies that strive solely for profit will fail.

NUMBERED REFERENCES

[1]Sabbath, 25b
[2]Avot, 3, 21
[3]Midrash, Exodus Rabbah 31:14
[4]Avot, 2, 8
[5]Avot, 3, 20
[6]Proverbs 30:7–9

Work as a Holy Act

Great is labor, for it gives honor to the worker.
—RABBI JUDAH[1]

In 2002, the Conference Board, a widely respected, not-for-profit organization established by corporate leaders in 1916 to find solutions to business problems that affect society, polled 5,000 U.S. households and found that only about half of those surveyed say they are happy in their jobs. This is down from 59 percent in 1995. The decline in job satisfaction is found among workers of all ages and across all income brackets.

The problem may be that we think about work in a way that makes it *impossible* to gain satisfaction from it. It's not the work itself that makes us unhappy; it's how we think about work that is the problem.

The Talmud offers a way of regarding labor that makes it satisfying, enjoyable, and fulfilling, no matter what we're doing or what we're being paid. This Talmudic understanding of work may be foreign to many of us, but it has brought solace and contentment to many people throughout the centuries.

The Holiness of Work

Judaism considers work a holy act because it is an emulation of God, who worked to create the earth and heavens. The Talmudic rabbis teach that the person who fears God is blessed; the person who eats as the result of his own labors is *twice* blessed. For a religion that stresses a belief in the absolute power of the Almighty, this teaching highlights the importance of work.

In many religions, blessings come as the result of prayer or good deeds. Although this is true for Jews, blessings also come from the simple act of work.

The Talmud's view of work is both spiritual *and* practical. People work for money to support themselves and their family. More important, having sufficient money enables people to spend time with their family and on other pleasurable pursuits.

There are those who express the desire to get more than money from their job or perhaps seek a measure of recognition or notice from their managers and coworkers. The Jewish tradition does not negate this need for acclaim, but it also does not encourage it. In Talmudic terms, work is its own reward. People work because it is the right thing to do—it brings them closer to God and provides a living. The simple act of going to work everyday helps all of those around us. Everyone should be concerned about their neighbors' well-being. A person's work, no matter how insignificant it may seem to the worker, contributes to the prosperity of the greater community. That's why Rabbi Judah remarked, "Great is labor, for it gives honor to the worker."

All Work Has Dignity

To the Talmudic rabbis, all work, no matter how unpleasant or humble, possesses dignity.

THE IMPORTANCE OF HAVING A SKILL, PART I

The ancient rabbis put great value on having a skill or trade on which people could depend for their livelihood. They were so passionate about the matter that their arguments often became heated. Rabbi Judah said, "He who does not teach his son a trade, teaches him to be a thief."[1] The other rabbis were somewhat amused at the ferocity of his statement, thinking perhaps he was being dramatic, but Rabbi Judah repeated his statement to make sure they all understood how strongly he felt about the matter.

The Hebrew word for trade or craft is *umanuth,* which can also be translated as "avocation" or "calling." The Talmudic rabbis knew that if people had a craft or trade, especially one that they could carry with them, they could always make a living. This fundamental concept in Jewish tradition may seem self-evident, but to a culture that was frequently forced to relocate, the ability to make a living from portable skills was tantamount to survival.

The notion that having a trade gives a person power arose during a lively discussion among Talmudic rabbis about the best ways to get people to tell the truth in court. They talked about threatening them, making sure they understood that God would punish them for lying by bringing a drought on their land. One rabbi noted that such punishment might succeed with some people but not with those who could earn a living no matter what befell them—that is, people with a trade. Rav Judah noted, "Though the drought lasted seven years, it never so much as passed the craftsman's house."[2]

[1]Kiddushin, 82b
[2]Sanhedrin, 29a

THE IMPORTANCE OF HAVING A SKILL, PART II

One of the Talmud's most poetic exchanges on the importance of having a skill was between Rabban Gamaliel and Rabbi Eleazar bar Zadok. Rabban Gamaliel said, "To what may he who has a craft be compared? To a vineyard encompassed by a hedge or to a ditch surrounded by a fence. But to what may he who has not craft be compared? To a vineyard not encompassed by a hedge, to a ditch not surrounded by a fence."

Rabbi Eleazar bar Zadok took this thought a step further, noting that having a skill amounts to lifetime security. He said, "To what may he who has a craft be likened? To a hedged vineyard into which neither cattle nor beast can enter; what is in it, no passerby can eat, and what is in it, no passerby can see. But to what may he who has no craft be compared? To a vineyard whose fence is breached. Cattle and beasts may enter it. Passersby can eat and see all that is in it."[1]

[1]Tosefta Kiddushin 1:11

A story is told in Jewish Scripture[2] about a well digger named Simeon who lived in the village of Sichnin. He once approached Rabbi Johannan ben Zakkai and said, "I am a well digger, but I am as great a man as you." The rabbi asked him how that could be so, and Simeon replied, "Because my work is as important to the community as yours. When you tell a man or woman to use water that is ceremonially purifying, I'm the one who has dug for it."

It may appear that Simeon's somewhat menial job could not possibly compare to the lofty position of a rabbi, but this is not so. The rabbi would not be able to accomplish his job if Simeon had not dug the well that produced the water for the purification ceremony. The lesson for us is that every job contributes to society in some way, even if it seems insignificant to us.

ARE SOME JOBS BETTER THAN OTHERS?

To the Talmudic rabbis, all work, no matter how unpleasant, possessed dignity. However, some counseled people to keep away from certain jobs such as those of ass drivers, camel drivers, sailors, and shepherds. These jobs presented the temptation to accept bribes and steal goods, and it was considered best to keep away from such temptation.

Other rabbis opposed this viewpoint, maintaining that, while these jobs may indeed offer temptation, this meant only that workers needed to be on guard. Moses, they argued, was both a shepherd *and* a righteous person.

The rabbis did mention one job that they thought was disagreeable, albeit necessary, because of its working environment: "The world cannot do without the perfumer and the tanner; but happy is he who is a perfumer by trade, and woe to him who is a tanner by trade."[1] Perfumeries smell nice, but tanneries are a different story.

[1]Kiddushin, 83b

The rabbis practiced what they preached, and all of them worked at other jobs, some of which might even be considered menial. Rabbi Akiva was a shepherd, Rabbi Hiyya bar Abin was a carpenter, Rabbi Abba bar Zmina was a tailor, and Rabbi Yitzak Nafha was a blacksmith. The rabbis esteemed manual labor because of its holiness, and the mix of jobs that they held contributes to the Talmud a range of opinions from various economic classes.

Don't Do It Just for the Money

The Talmud argues that high-paying and distinguished professions should not be entered into solely because of their trappings. Not everyone is happy doing them or succeeds in getting rich. Rabbi Meir warned us: "... for in every trade and pursuit of life there are rich and poor to be found. It is folly for one to say, 'this is a bad trade, it will not afford me a living,' because he will find many doing well in the same occupation. Neither should a successful man boast and say 'this is a great trade, a glorious art, it has made me wealthy,' because many working in that occupation have found poverty."[3] Meir concluded that the distinction was not in the work but in the person doing it.

A good example is the profession of physician, traditionally considered to bring not only financial gain but social status as well. However, many contemporary Western doctors are growing dissatisfied. Certainly the increase in bureaucracy and other nonmedical issues with which they must contend is a contributing factor to their unhappiness. Furthermore, many doctors simply are not earning the high salaries and degree of respect that previous generations of doctors enjoyed and that the younger doctors expected to receive, too.

On the other hand, family practice doctors whose motivation for being physicians is benevolence rather than money or prestige feel greater job satisfaction, according to a survey published in the March 2000 issue of the *Archives of Family Medicine.* Acts of benevolence ranged from training the next generation of physicians to treating underinsured patients.

WORK IS ONE OF LIFE'S MYSTERIES

Work is given such prominence in people's lives that it's ranked with the other great mysteries of existence. The Talmudic rabbis listed seven things that are hidden from people and are thus mysterious: the day of death, judgment by God, what is in a neighbor's heart, when the Messiah would come, when our day of "consolation" will arrive, when the "wicked kingdom" (probably referring to the then-current Roman Empire) would come to an end, and how a person would earn a living.

The lesson for all of us is that we should not choose a job or profession only on the basis of the financial remuneration or prestige that comes with it. Too many people take jobs they dislike in the hope of acquiring status or wealth. These people would never have attained peace in the world of the Talmudic rabbis, and they aren't likely to attain peace in our contemporary world, either.

What If a Person Is Rich Enough Not to Work?

The Talmud teaches that even if a man provides his wife with a hundred servants, she must still do some of the housework herself. Idleness could lead to "lewdness" and "mental instability," according to the rabbis. In contemporary terms, we would translate this to mean that working keeps us centered and out of trouble.

William Julius Wilson, a sociology professor at the University of Chicago and author of *The Truly Disadvantaged: The Inner City, The Underclass and Public Policy* (University of Chicago, 1990), echoes the Talmud's opinion on work. Speaking at Boston College in February 1994, Wilson noted, "Regular employment provides an anchor for the central, spatial aspects of life. In the absence of regular employment, life—including family life—becomes incoherent." He added, "Neighborhoods plagued with high levels of joblessness are more likely to experience the problems of social organization."

Studies performed by Wilson and others have shown that people who work, no matter what their job, feel more in control of their lives and more respectable. The tendency is to think this has do with making money, but that's only part of it. Having a job gives people a sense of accomplishment and purpose. Working binds people to their neighborhoods and communities, making them part of a larger family.

One reason that our Western culture has been slow to recognize the sacred nature and nobility of work is that our attitudes toward work have been heavily influenced by ancient Greek and Roman culture, in which wealth was sought so people would *not* have to work anymore. The idleness and leisure afforded by wealth were a sign that a person was a member of the aristocracy. Wealth was therefore a means to a refined and genteel lifestyle, free of work and obligations.

A LEGACY THROUGH WORK

"The merit of work stands by a man where the merits of his ancestors cannot."[1]

This passage makes the point that the legacy we leave through our work is greater than anything our parents left to us that we in turn passed on to others after our death. It also is a call to those who have been blessed with wealth from birth to make their own way in the world and not simply build on what was presented to them.

[1]Tanhuma Va-yetze 13 (an early medieval Midrash)

The Talmudic Cure for Work-Related Stress

Overwork is an epidemic in modern society. In a 2001 study conducted by the New York–based, nonprofit Families and Work Institute, 46 percent of respondents said they felt overworked in some way, 28 percent said they were overwhelmed by their workload, and 29 percent said they had no time to step back and reflect on their work. Almost one-quarter of U.S. workers said they spent 50 or more hours on the job weekly, 22 percent said they worked six to seven days a week, and 25 percent said they didn't use vacation time to which they were entitled. The average American worker today rarely takes the traditional two-weeks' vacation of their parents' generation. Instead, they break up vacation time into mini-vacations, adding a day or two to weekends and holidays and spreading them throughout the year. Even when workers are away from the office, many remain in touch through laptop computers and cell phones.

People overwork for many reasons. Some people are obsessed with performing their jobs perfectly. Others enjoy being at work so much that they lose track of time. Some, sadly, prefer being at work to being at home because they feel more successful there than in their family environment.

Most often, however, people overwork because they have been forced to do so by the massive layoffs of the past several years. These so-called ghost workers—those remaining after the layoffs—are forced to take up the slack and compensate for those who have been dismissed. Not only are they doing more work because of the lower number of remaining workers, but ghost workers often work longer hours, hoping to impress their boss into keeping them on the payroll if another round of layoffs occurs.

Aside from the human and spiritual side of the problem, there's a practical hazard from overwork. The pace of business is constantly increasing, and with the world careening toward a 24-hour economy, work and other obligations are cutting into people's sleep time. Most Americans sleep one hour a night less than they should, and fatigue is cited as a major contributor to workplace errors and accidents.

A December 2002 report from the Harvard School of Public Health and the Henry J. Kaiser Family Foundation, a national health philanthropic group, showed that more than two in five patients and one-third of doctors responding to a survey said they or their family members have experienced medical errors, some of which caused injury or death to patients. Of the reasons given for these errors, 72 percent cited doctors not spending enough time with patients. Overwork, stress, or fatigue on the part of health professionals came in a close second, at 70 percent.

In 1997, after a series of accidents—one of which killed seven people—involving the nation's largest railroad, Union Pacific, Federal Rail Administration chief Jolene M. Molitoris said that preliminary results of a safety inspection showed fatigue caused by overwork to be the main reason behind dangerous train maneuvers, dispatcher errors, and missing freight information.

"You have people who are working 7 days a week, 12-plus hours a day with no time off. When you are that tired it makes top performance and safety assurance impossible," she said. "And that schedule isn't just for a week or so, it's constant."

While fatigue and burnout can cause fatal accidents involving those in the health, transportation, and similar high-risk industries, it can lower productivity in other industries. An office worker's errors may not result in loss of life, but they can cost companies money and time.

According to a 2001 study by the International Labor Organization in Geneva, Switzerland, despite the long hours American workers are putting in, American productivity grew by only 22 percent between 1980 and 1996, compared to 30 percent or more in Europe and 43 percent in Japan, two countries in which workers worked fewer hours.

The Sabbath

We can take some solace in knowing that the problem of overwork is not unique to our era. The Talmudic rabbis were well aware of its dangers. Not only did too much work steal time from family and community, but it took time away from studies. Jewish life stresses the importance of maintaining an equilibrium between work and other activities. Too much of either one, and life is out of balance.

A cure for much of the modern stress, fatigue, and overwork can be found in the simple idea of a Sabbath, once a radical notion that was codified for the first time by Jewish law in the Ten Commandments. Before the institution of a Sabbath, people worked at the whim of their superiors, and they worked seven days a week. There was no time to rest or pursue leisure activities.

A cure for much of the modern stress, fatigue, and overwork can be found in the simple idea of a Sabbath, once a radical notion that was codified for the first time by Jewish law in the Ten Commandments.

Everyone, regardless of religious beliefs, needs the equivalent of a Sabbath to recharge mentally, physically, and spiritually. They should remove themselves from their day-to-day work lives. Simply taking a day off for rejuvenation bestows immediate benefits on the individual, his family, and the workplace.

My friend Bob Meyers, a former journalist and president of the National Press Foundation, was raised Jewish but was not observant. Several years ago, he became interested in organized Judaism. He started lighting Sabbath candles and reciting prayers over bread and

BALANCE, ALWAYS BALANCE

"Study, combined with a secular occupation is a fine thing, for the double labor makes sin to be forgotten. All study [of the Torah] with which no work goes, will in the end come to naught, and bring sin in its train."[1]

The ancient rabbis continually emphasized moderation in all endeavors. Although it is tempting to study as much as possible so you will be revered for your knowledge, too much studying will lead to an out-of-balance life. Study must be combined with outside labor in order to lead a righteous existence. One of the ancillary benefits of work is that it takes up time that might be spent on other pursuits that, if unchecked, could become all-consuming.

[1]Mishnah Kiddushin, 1, 10

wine. He read and studied Jewish texts. At the same time, he began taking the concept of a day of rest seriously. "I stopped doing simple things like answering the phone, which immediately disconnected me from the outside world," said Meyers. "I found myself becoming more peaceful. I thought about things. The Sabbath became my island in time." Meyers found that observing the Sabbath allowed him to bring a new intensity to both his religious life and his work life.

The idea behind a Sabbath or day of rest was to break the work cycle and offer a much-needed respite—even work animals were given a day of rest. But the ancient Hebrews had an idea that went even further: the sabbatical.

The Sabbatical

The sabbatical was part of the ancient Hebrew's cycle of seven. The Sabbath occurred every seventh day, and the sabbatical year occurred every seventh year. All indentured servants were freed in the seventh year. There was also a *jubilee* year, which fell every seventh sabbatical year, or every 49 years. During the jubilee year, all land reverted to its original owners. Since land was the main source of wealth, the jubilee year ensured that no one became rich for too long a period. This also reinforced the notion that all land belonged to God and could not be sold in perpetuity. Spiritually, the jubilee year signified starting over, but the more frequent sabbatical years also signaled a renewal of spirit and life course.

Once the sole province of college professors, about 10 percent of large U.S. firms now offer formal sabbatical or leave-of-absence programs, while many others practice some form of the sabbatical, according to the Conference Board. The proportion of firms offering some type of leave is expected to reach one-third during this decade.

Well-known companies offering sabbatical programs include McDonald's, Du Pont, American Express, Xerox, Tandem, IBM, and

SABBATICAL EXPERIENCES

McDonald's Corporation believes that offering sabbaticals reaps benefits for both the company and its employees, and has had a sabbatical plan in force since 1978. One of the company's top employees, Barry Mehrman, had postponed his sabbatical for four years after his eligibility for it, because he had just relocated his family to Chicago. The year after he returned from his sabbatical, Mehrman's productivity earned him the president's award, bestowed on the top 1 percent of the McDonald's global workforce. "I was charged up when I came back to work and feeling great about myself. I was able to perform at such a high level, because I had time to think about my vision for work while I was off," Mehrman told *Restaurant Business* magazine (January 20, 1996), which studied sabbaticals in the restaurant industry.

Silicon Graphics officials allow workers to use their six-week's time off for any purpose, and they report that their employees return refreshed, full of energy, and brimming with new ideas. One woman spent the time overcoming her fear of skiing. She returned to work more confident about herself and her ability to manage.

Even the elite take time off. Management guru Tom Peters recently returned from his sabbatical year, and country superstar Garth Brooks took a two-year hiatus to be with his family and reflect on his quick rise to stardom. Peters reported that he has more ideas than before, and Brooks didn't miss a beat when he returned.

Silicon Graphics. The Conference Board found that sabbaticals were most common in high-tech firms, consulting companies, and law firms—jobs that tend to have high worker burnout rates. Many Silicon Valley companies use sabbaticals to entice scarce workers into industries where they strain to push products and services to market at breakneck speed. Intel, for example, provides an eight-week sabbatical, with full salary, after each seven years of full-time service.

Do Sabbaticals Work?

Leaving the land fallow during the ancient sabbatical year enabled it to produce more and larger crops in subsequent years. The same principle can be applied to worker sabbaticals: People return refreshed and ready to be more productive.

The benefits of sabbaticals cannot be easily quantified, but strong anecdotal evidence points to their payback. Morningstar, Inc., the mutual fund tracking company, has a commitment to sabbaticals, offering employees six weeks off every four years. Discussing sabbaticals in the *Wall Street Journal,* CEO Don Phillips noted, "People may get to certain points in their careers where they are responding to day-to-day concerns and forget the big picture. The sabbatical lets them get perspective."

HARD WORK ALWAYS PAYS OFF

"If a person says to you: 'I have worked and have not achieved,' do not believe that person.

"If the person says: 'I have not worked but still I have achieved,' do not believe that person.

"But if the person says: 'I have worked and I have achieved,' you may believe that person."[1]

[1]Megillah, 6a

The concept of the sabbatical year worked for the ancient Hebrews for two main reasons. Each person devised a plan to use the year for study, and it was something they looked forward to and desired. Second, there was an underlying faith in God and in themselves that when they returned, they would be wiser and better equipped spiritually and intellectually to work at their regular tasks.

Many contemporary workers would like to take a sabbatical, but they are afraid of being out of step when they return. The solution to this is to build faith in yourself and in your abilities. The faith of the ancient Jews came largely from the Talmudic notion that God would provide sustenance based on individual effort. If people were willing to work hard, they could always succeed.

Working in One's Own Business

In ancient times, most workers were day laborers who gathered in one area, perhaps the marketplace, hoping to work in a field, at a building construction site, or in some other labor-intensive occupation. Landowners sought the strongest, most skilled laborers and gave them work for the day or, if the laborer was fortunate, for a longer period. It was an especially difficult way to make a living because the worker could never count on finding work on a given day.

Knowing how hard it was to be a day laborer, sometimes toiling at the whim of a cruel boss, the Talmudic rabbis recommended that people try to work for themselves—to start their own business. This is one reason for the healthy entrepreneurialism among Jews. Another reason is that anti-Semitism kept Jews out of many jobs. The uniqueness of the religion sets Jews apart, so making a living without having to depend on others is a valued ability.

Rabbi Ahai ben Josiah said, "He who eats of his own is as much at ease as an infant raised at his mother's breast. When a man eats of his own, his mind is at ease. But a man's mind is not at ease when he eats even at his father's table, his mother's table or his children's table, let alone a stranger's table."[4]

The rabbis were so adamant about self-reliance through work that they believed it was better to work at a job outside of your expertise rather than not work at all. "Sell yourself to work that is alien to you rather than depend on the handouts of others," they advised.[5] Although they didn't advocate faking your way into a job, they applauded those who were willing to take a less skilled position if it meant they could be independent.

Summary—Lesson Two

1. Work is considered a holy act, and all work has intrinsic dignity, no matter what the job.

2. The main practical purpose of work is to earn money. However, work also builds self-esteem by allowing people to support themselves, their family, and the community. Work is our contribution to those around us.

3. A day of rest during the week is necessary for a person's all-around well-being. It increases productivity as well.

4. Strike a balance between work and leisure. Too much of either is harmful.

NUMBERED REFERENCES

[1]Nedarim, 49b
[2]Ecclesiastes 4:17
[3]Kiddushin, 82a
[4]Rabbi Ahai ben Josiah, from the Avot de-Rabbi Natan
[5]Rabbi Akiva, Palestinian Talmud, Berakot 9:3, 13d

Treating Workers Well Pays Dividends

*He who wishes to lose money should hire workers
and not direct them.*

—RABBI YOHANNAN[1]

To the Talmudic rabbis, the relationship between employee and employer is tantamount to a contract between two independent parties, each with specific rights and obligations to the other.

The governing concept is this: A worker agrees to work, and the employer agrees to pay for that work. This is not as simple an idea as it may first appear, especially in today's complex business environment. For employers, it means providing leadership, offering guidance, paying wages promptly, honoring local customs, providing a safe environment, preserving the workplace, giving equitable treatment, and rendering a fair share of taxes. For workers, it means understanding workplace rights, not taking advantage of breaks, coming to work on time ready to do one's best, being honest about looking for new employment, and not taking even the cheapest office supply for personal use.

The Talmudic rabbis spent more time discussing an employer's obligations and responsibilities than those of their employees, given the business owner's often superior economic position. The rabbis made certain, though, that workers clearly understood their accountability to the company as well.

Leadership Traits

What makes a great leader?, the Talmudic rabbis wondered.

They were curious why so many great Hebrew leaders had been shepherds and goatherds earlier in life—Moses being the major example, but also King David as a youth. In Psalms 11:5, young David first led the lambs to pasture to eat the tender grass, then the older ones to eat stiffer grass, then the mature sheep to eat coarse grass. According to legend, this caring and compassion for each individual sheep showed God that David could lead the Lord's flock when he grew older.

Likewise, Moses was tending his father-in-law's flock when a young goat ran away. Moses followed it and watched as the kid found a spring and drank. Moses said, "I didn't know that your thirst made you run away. You are tired and I will carry you back."

After some discussion, the rabbis understood that the best herders exhibited compassion and sensitivity toward their flock, especially for the weaker animals. The most successful herders knew each animal's habits and routines and treated each one individually. These, the rabbis said, were the characteristics of a strong and just leader.

Along with compassion, leaders must possess steadfast resolve and logic in order to make difficult decisions and choices. Ben Zoma asked, "Who is a leader? One who conquers one's passions and emotions."[2] They must also maintain control of their emotions: "When the shepherd is enraged at the flock, he blinds the eyes of the bellwether."[3] The bellwether is the male sheep who wears a bell around his neck and leads the flock according to the shepherd's commands. When the shepherd loses his temper, the bellwether becomes confused and doesn't know where to head next. So, too, if a company leader loses his temper or behaves irrationally, the employees are at loose ends, with no guidance for going forward.

THE DOWNSIDE OF BEING A LEADER

"The years of him are shortened who runs after leadership. Why did Joseph die before his brothers?" the rabbis asked. "Because he was masterful and ruled over them."[1]

In this famous story from Scripture, Joseph was the twelfth son of Jacob, who favored him above his brothers. This made Joseph's brothers jealous—and even more so after Joseph dreamed that he and his brothers were bundling stalks of corn and his brothers' bundles bowed to his bundle. In another dream, Joseph saw the sun and moon and 11 stars (the 11 other sons) bow before him.

Because they were jealous of his leadership position, the brothers decided to get rid of Joseph. They threw him into an empty well, after tearing off his coat of many colors, which their father had given him. They returned home and lied to their father, saying that Joseph had been killed by an animal. Joseph was found by a caravan and taken to Egypt as a prisoner.

Joseph's abilities again revealed themselves as he interpreted the Pharaoh's dream of seven fat cows eating seven skinny cows to represent seven good years and seven lean years. The Pharaoh was so impressed that he appointed Joseph as the leader who would store food for the famine years. Joseph was appointed governor of Egypt.

Although he later was reunited with his father and brothers—and he forgave them for their actions against him—the stressful tasks of leadership took their toll on Joseph, and he died before his brothers.

[1]Berakot, 55

The Talmud stresses that a group's behavior comes from the top: "The acts of the leader are the acts of the nation. If the leader is just, the nation is just; if the leader is unjust, that nation is also unjust and will be punished for the sins of the leader."[4] The term *nation* applies to any group of people, including companies.

Unfortunately, in recent years the behavior of certain leaders has tainted the reputations of their employees. Workers at accounting and consulting firm Arthur Andersen were punished for the sins of their leaders—by losing their jobs as a result of the illegal behavior of managers who ordered the shredding of documents concerning their client Enron. (Andersen also had been the object of Securities and Exchange Commission actions a year earlier, in 2001, for questionable audits of its clients Sunbeam and Waste Management.) In her 2003 book *Final Accounting: Ambition, Greed and the Fall of Arthur Andersen* (Broadway Books, 2003), Barbara Ley Toffler, a former ethics consultant at the company and now adjunct professor of management at Columbia's graduate business school, noted: "It was a culture in which everyone followed the rules of the leader. When the rules and leaders stood for decency and integrity, the lock step culture was the key to competence and respectability. But when the game and the leaders changed direction, the culture of conformity led to disaster."

Enron employees also suffered because of the illegal and immoral activities of its leaders. Not only were they punished financially by losing their jobs and, in some cases, their life savings (which were in company stock), they were punished emotionally because the trust they had in their leaders was shattered. If we expand the "nation" concept a bit further to include outside shareholders, it's clear that many more people have been similarly financially punished as a result of the sins of these disreputable company leaders.

Another characteristic of successful leaders is that they must be consensus builders, able to work with those who disagree with their point of view. "Who is the leader of all leaders? Some say the one who makes an enemy into one's friend."[5]

When companies experience crises and disarray due to internal clashes, consensus builders are often brought in to mend fences. For instance, Richard Parsons, an AOL Time Warner chief operating officer, was named the company's CEO in 2002 because of his long history of political involvement and a knack for consensus building. He took control at a time when the AOL merger with Time Warner was starting to unravel and rivalries between the older, more established media giant Time Warner and the less profitable, Internet-based AOL were reaching fever pitch. AOL cofounder Steve Case, who remained as chairman, said in a public statement, "Dick [Parsons] has exactly the right style of leadership, understanding of people, ability to build alliances and commitment to serve the public interest that is critical for the company."

The Talmud reminds leaders not to become arrogant, because conceit leads to mistakes and a loss of spiritual grounding. "Woe to high position, for it takes the fear of heaven from the person who occupies it."[6]

An arrogant leader is more than an annoyance to those who work with him or her—such an attitude can cost a company dearly. In his book *Mergers & Acquisitions: Managing the Transaction* (McGraw-Hill, 1997), Joseph Krallinger says, "Overpaying is the worst and most frequent mistake made by buyers." He argues that this error is mainly due to arrogance on the part of the purchaser. Some CEOs and other decision makers believe they can pay a high price for a property and then compensate with their stellar managerial skills, which, in their minds, can overcome any obstacle. In *Valuation for M&A: Building Value in Private Companies,* Frank C. Evans and David M. Bishop comment that "the average acquisition premium paid for public companies above their fair market value has been about 40% over the last ten years." They conclude that "acquiring managers' egos frequently outpace their logic…bidding managers infected with [exaggerated pride or self-confidence] overestimate their ability to manage the [acquisition] and hence overpay for it."

The rabbis also discussed the importance of self-interest because they believed it to be a prime factor in business success in general and in leadership in particular. In *Wealth of Nations* (1776), economist Adam Smith argued for what he termed "enlightened self-interest," which urges leaders to strive for profits, for the benefit of society, but without hurting others in the process. This "enlightened" view of self-interest is what the rabbis had in mind.

They tell the story of a man who is looking for an article he lost and an article that his father lost. The rabbis agree that the man should look for his own lost item first. Is this being selfish? The rabbis contend that people should look after their own needs first before taking care of others' needs. "There shall be no neediness in you," said Rabbi Judah, which implies that you should take care of yourself first. They add that unless you take care of yourself first, you may not be able to help others. Rabbi Judah continued, "He who takes care of others' needs first, will eventually become poverty stricken."[7] Another rabbi concurred: "Wash yourself, before washing others."[8]

Those of us who fly may be struck by the warning from airline attendants to place the oxygen mask over our own face before helping others with theirs. This is especially difficult for parents, who instinctively want to place the mask over their children's faces first, even though that would actually be counterproductive.

Hillel summed up this discussion when he said, "If I am not for myself, who will be for me? And if I am only for myself, what am I? And if not now, when?"[9] Aside from the matter of self-interest stated here, Hillel is also calling for us to conquer our own temptations to be selfish. He urges us to seize opportunity as it comes, or it may disappear forever. "While the fire is burning, slice your pumpkin and fry it."[10]

Important qualities for leaders are optimism and the self-confidence that they can achieve greatness. They must have faith that their future is in their hands and that they have the power to shape their destiny through hard work and perseverance. In this regard, the Talmudic rabbis were adamant about the importance of free will. They believed that although God ordains our future, we nevertheless have the freedom to control our own individual lives. This is not as contradictory as it seems. Because we do not know in advance *what* our destiny will be, we have the ability to set a course for ourselves. As Rabbi Akiva noted, "Everything is foreseen and freedom of choice is given and the world is judged with goodness. Everything depends on how hard you work."[11]

A related passage reinforces the idea that our fate is ours to shape: "Whoever desires to soil himself with sin will find all the gates open to him. Whoever wants to attain the highest purity will find that all the forces of purity are ready to help him."[12] This is similar to Henry Ford's famous quote: "If you think you can do a thing or think you can't do a thing, you're right."

Local Laws and Customs Prevail

One of the basic assertions that govern all business activities, especially employers' obligations, is that local laws and customs always should prevail. The ancient rabbis applied this to worker wages and benefits and asked a basic question: What if an employer were to hire workers and not specify exactly when they were to come to work or how long they were to work, but after they were hired insist that they stay late or come in early?

The Talmudic rabbis said that workers would not be required to work extra hours unless it was the local norm to do so. The same would hold for workers who received dinner when they worked late or free tea during the day. If it was the local custom to receive such perks, then the employer must provide them. In our modern society, local custom could mean a company-wide convention in the case of huge corporations, or it could mean citywide norms in some urban areas. For example, people in cities like Washington, D.C., and New York regularly work late—even pride themselves on how late they work—while employees in Denver and San Francisco tend to leave work earlier.

LOCAL CUSTOMS PREVAIL

"Where it is the custom to feed workers, you must feed them. Where it is the custom to supply them with a dessert after meals you must do so. All should be according to local custom."[1]

The rabbis wanted to ensure that workers were treated according to local customs, even if it meant detailing the exact meals they were to be fed. They often went into long discussions about the types of beans or vegetables that were to be supplied by the employer. The idea of following local customs is a hallmark of Talmudic thought and extends to all types of daily practices. The main reason that rabbis were insistent on following local rules is that Jewish populations were dispersed over many lands, and it was important that they fit in with their surroundings and become part of their communities.

[1]Bava Metzia, 7a

What about companies that operate factories in developing countries and pay what we would consider extremely low wages? The Talmud would argue that local custom should dictate wages and working conditions. However, this does not apply if working conditions are harsh or unhealthy or if workers and employers do not have parity in their contract negotiations.

In one of the most-often-quoted passages on the matter of employer obligation, the rabbis argued vigorously about just how far an employer must go in implementing local customs.

Rabbi Yohannan ben Matya said to his son, "Go out and hire workers for us." The son did as he was told. The son agreed that workers would get food, but he did not specify how much or what kind. When the son returned and told his father the arrangement he had made, the father became very upset. "My son, I cannot accept this agreement.

Even if you prepare the most lavish meal for these workers, like a feast befitting King Solomon in his time, you would not have fulfilled your obligation to these workers."[13]

The rabbi instructed his son to find the workers and tell them that they would work only for bread and beans, because it was the local custom to supply workers with such food. "But you must do it quickly," the rabbi said, "because after they begin work it will be impossible to make any further changes in our agreement with them. The act of beginning work finalizes the labor contract."

The other rabbis argued over Rabbi Yohannan ben Matya's situation. Rabban Shimon ben Gamaliel said that it wasn't necessary to inform the workers of their exact food allotment; local custom meant providing bread and beans. He said that Rabbi Yohannan ben Matya was not obliged to give the workers any more than that.

The Gemara took this a step further. If an employer said during negotiations that he would pay a prospective worker more than the prevailing wage, he must specify what he wants in return. The rabbis pointed out that a worker could fairly say he thought the higher wages were for better-quality work. The worker would not necessarily assume that the additional money was for working extra hours if that was not the local custom.

The practice of working extra hours has become a hot issue among employees these days. Many people would prefer to spend more time with their families in the evenings but are prevented from doing so by peer and supervisor pressure to stay later at the office. Some become resentful and may feel blindsided by not having been told in advance that they were expected to stay late or work weekends. Tensions can grow between younger workers who don't have families and older workers who do.

Prospective workers and employers must have a clear understanding of what they expect from each other before entering into an employment agreement. This consensus on the terms of employment is both a righteous act and a profitable one. Workers are happiest and most productive when they know exactly what they are to do, and employers make more money when their wishes are carried out. This is the idea behind Rabbi Yohannan's admonition: "He who wishes to lose money should hire workers and not direct them."

Prospective workers and employers must have a clear understanding of what they expect from each other before entering into an employment agreement.

Pay Wages Promptly

The Talmudic rabbis discussed how and when salaries were to be paid. At that time, employers were obligated to pay day laborers that same day before sunset because that was when the day's work was done.

The rabbis also specified that a worker must be paid in local currency and not in goods. One Talmudic story concerns a farmer who hired a day laborer to help gather straw and tie it into bundles. When the worker requested his wages, the farmer offered him straw instead of money. The worker insisted that he be paid with money, and the rabbis concurred.

What about being paid in company stock instead of money? The Talmud would seem to prohibit such a transaction because stock is not currency. In recent years, the practice at many start-up companies has been to supplement employees' wages with stock options—which may constitute the local custom. According to the Talmud, this would be permitted only if it was agreed to prior to the employee's starting work. However, if the worker was expecting a paycheck but the employer wanted to pay him in stock because the company was unable to make its payroll, that would not be acceptable.

The Mouse and the Hole

Managers and business owners must know what's going on in all parts of their companies and impose controls and procedures to prevent profit-stealing activities. This is not just good business procedure but an *obligation*.

The Talmud tells the story of Rabbi Abaye, who took this obligation seriously and made it a practice to inspect his fields daily. One day he came upon a tenant farmer who didn't recognize Abaye as the master of the property. The tenant was carrying some vine shoots, and Abaye asked him where he was taking them. "To the master's house," he lied. Abaye replied, "The sages anticipated you a long time ago." This is a Talmudic tongue-in-cheek way of saying that there will always be people who try to steal because they think no one is watching.[14]

The Talmudic rabbis said that if a manager or business owner was not paying attention, then he should not be surprised if employees and others stole from him. Extending the discussion, they raised the question of whether an employer actually *encouraged* workers to steal from him if he did not pay attention. (It's not politically correct these days to blame the victim for the crime, but the Talmud is not always politically correct by contemporary standards.)

In Jewish Scripture, Leviticus talks about the wrongness of "putting stumbling blocks before a blind person," a literal instance of causing an impaired person to trip and get hurt. The Talmud expands this precise prohibition to preventing someone from incurring injury through inaction as well—for instance, not alerting someone who is about to enter into a bad business deal. The key is whether your intentions are honest. This is a recurring theme in the Talmud and has a wide range of applications, especially those involving consumer protection and advertising.

The story of the mouse and the hole is a classic piece of Jewish lore that illustrates this theme. (This story is also told as the goat and a broken fence, but the idea is the same.) A mouse walked through a hole in the wall and ate some food. Who was to blame for the missing food?

55

One rabbi argued that the mouse was to blame because it ate the food. The other rabbi argued that if not for the hole, there would be no mouse in the house; therefore, the hole, and not the mouse, was to blame for the food theft.

MY BOSS MADE ME DO IT

"If a worker has discharged his appointed errand, the employer is guilty of sacrilege, but if he has not carried out his appointed errand, he himself is guilty of sacrilege. For instance: if the employer said: give flesh to the guests and he offered them liver, or liver and he offered them flesh, he himself is guilty of sacrilege. If the employer said to him: 'give them one piece each,' and he said to them: 'take two pieces each,' while the guests themselves took three pieces each, all of them are guilty of sacrilege."[1]

The Talmud is very clear on the subject of culpability when it involves acts at work. Here, the rabbis say that if the employer tells the worker to engage in an illegal act and the worker refuses, then the employer is at fault. If the worker engages in an illegal act on his own, without the employer's knowledge, then only the worker is at fault. However, if the employer gives an illegal order and the employee carries it out, then both are acting illegally. This last instance is sometimes at odds with modern situations in which a worker engages in an illegal act, such as bribery, because his boss told him to do so. Indeed, in such a case, the client who takes the bribe would be considered guilty, as well. To the ancient rabbis, carrying out an illegal act because you were ordered to do so by a superior is no defense against prosecution. This stands in contrast to contemporary courts, which sometimes show leniency toward workers in such situations.

[1]Mishna Mas. Me'ilah, 20a

Rabbis argued both sides with great fervor; however, the main point is that to place temptation in someone's path—especially if the person is weak—is tantamount to stealing the item yourself. This does not mean that the rabbis were permanently cynical about their fellow man, assuming that people would always steal if given an opportunity. Rather, the Talmudic sages believed that *all* of us are capable of poor judgment at times, and it's best not to put ourselves in the way of tempting situations.

To be sure, the rabbis would never go so far as to say that a victim of a street assault was asking for it by being out on a certain street, but even law enforcement agencies suggest that people should pick their travel routes judiciously.

Victor Jacobs, chief executive of Allou Health & Beauty Care, believes in running his company according to many of the Talmudic precepts. He has paid special attention to the story of the mouse and the hole.

Since his pharmaceutical distribution company went public in 1989, sales have climbed from $71 million to almost $400 million, and profits have quadrupled to $4 million. In a very low-margin business, Allou's 4.2 percent margins are double those of its closest competitors.

Without reservation, Jacobs credits the Talmud with his company's success. "It opens your mind and teaches you how to think. It gives you the best practical business advice anywhere," he told *Fortune* magazine in 1994.

Because its pharmaceutical products were so easily fenced on the black market, Allou was losing 40 cartons of merchandise a week. Realizing that the goods were just too tempting for thieves to pass up, Jacobs planned to "plug the hole so the mice couldn't get in." The company decided to shrink-wrap the goods before shipment. The incidence of theft dropped immediately to less than one carton a month. Simple solution? Yes, but Allou was the first company in its industry to do this.

Contemporary Talmudic scholars have been discussing the case of Nick Leeson, who was tried, convicted, and imprisoned for engaging in highly speculative and fraudulent trades in the Japanese and Singapore futures exchanges that cost Barings bank $1.4 billion and ultimately caused its collapse. How could such a thing happen? Rabbi Pinchas Rosenstein, director of the Jewish Association for Business Ethics in the United Kingdom, wrote in the organization's newsletter: "Placing a stumbling block before the blind has never been limited to its purely literal meaning. This concept is considered a prohibition on placing people in contexts where they would be unable to cope with their responsibilities and temptation. This point takes on a greater relevance as it appears that adequate systems of financial control were simply non-existent in the Barings case, whereby one individual was allowed to control both the front and back offices, a situation that inevitably led to abuse."

Rosenstein and others pointed out that the ancient Hebrew priests who entered the Temple treasury were forbidden to wear cloaks with long sleeves, so they could never be accused of hiding coins or gold to take outside. This practice of wearing short sleeves put them above suspicion by removing temptation from their path. "Indeed, even the greatest Jewish leader of all times, Moses, was expected to provide a full set of accounts relating to raw materials donated for the construction of the Tabernacle," Rosenstein noted.

These examples are not meant to suggest that all employees can be swayed by circumstances into illegal or immoral actions, but they constitute recognition by the Talmudic rabbis that human beings are always tempted by money and subject to momentary lapses in judgment.

What If It's Nobody's Fault?

What happens if a worker comes to work and there is nothing for him to do? If it is the owner's fault, should the worker be paid anyway, or is the worker simply out of luck?

This discussion is relevant to contemporary workers at dot-coms and other speculative companies that can be here one day and gone the next. What are owners' and managers' obligations in such circumstances?

A Talmudic story revolves around a group of day laborers who showed up expecting fieldwork. The night before, however, it had rained and the fields were now flooded.

THE VALUE OF A WORKER'S LIFE

Readers are often impressed with the Talmud's recognition of the sanctity and importance of work, and how often work is compared to life itself. "Whoever withholds an employee's wages, it is as if he has taken the person's life from him."[1]

This is especially true in the following passage, in which the Talmudic rabbis implore employers to pay wages promptly and fairly, especially for jobs in which the worker literally risks his life for money: "The rabbis said to the employer: 'This poor man ascends the highest scaffold, climbs the highest trees. For what does he expose himself to such danger if not to make a living? Be careful, not to oppress him in his wages, for it means his very life.' "[2]

[1]Bava Metzia, 112a
[2]Sifre Ki Tetze, sec. 279, p. 123b

The rabbis vacillated about this one. Some said that the workers were entitled to their wages because it wasn't their fault that the fields were flooded. Others argued that it wasn't the owner's fault, either, and he should not have to pay for work that couldn't be done due to an act of nature. The rabbis debated further and reached a conclusion. The answer lay in who knew what and when.

The rabbis argued that if both the workers and the farm owner had surveyed the land the previous evening and each of them had understood the conditions, then the workers took on the job at their own risk. Specifically, if the workers understood that the river often overflowed the fields, that it was the time of year during which this might occur, or that it was already near flood stage, then they took the job knowing that the river might overflow during the night and there would be no work the next morning.

On the other hand, if the owner knew that the river often overflowed at this time of year and didn't mention it to the laborers, then this owner should pay the workers for a day's labor regardless of whether they actually worked.

An analogous situation would exist today for employees of a company in perilous financial condition. An employer who continued to hype the company's prospects, knowing all the while that it was in dire straits, would be in the wrong. However, an employer who informs employees of the risks allows the workers to make their own decisions and thus fulfills his moral obligation to them.

Although the Talmud makes it clear that an employer is under no obligation to pay workers if employees take on a job at their own risk, it does not prohibit such payment. The Talmudic rabbis made a strong case for taking care of workers who must live from paycheck to paycheck. To do so would be to go beyond the law, exceeding the level of piety and kindness it requires.

Aaron Feuerstein, owner of Malden Mills, was under no specific Talmudic ruling to continue paying his workers after his facility burned down. No one could have anticipated the fire. However, the Talmudic rabbis were not always interested in the letter of the law; they were more interested in the spirit of the law. In Feuerstein's case, rebuilding his mills and paying his workers were consistent with the

WORKPLACE PRESERVATION: MALDEN MILLS

Employers are obligated to do everything they can to keep their businesses operating and profitable so they can provide employment and build community prosperity. Witness Aaron Feuerstein's actions when his plant burned down.

Feuerstein owns Malden Mills, a textile factory complex located in the Boston suburb of Lawrence, Massachusetts. When fire destroyed the mill on December 11, 1995, its employees prepared themselves for the inevitable outcome. Many workers had already spent large portions of their recent paychecks on Christmas gifts. They figured they would now cash their last check and head for the unemployment office.

But Feuerstein did something so unusual that President Clinton was moved to invite him to sit with his wife Hillary and daughter Chelsea during the State of the Union address the following month. The 70-year-old Feuerstein decided to keep all 3,000 workers on the payroll and pay their medical benefits until the 90-year-old family business could be rebuilt. He paid workers for January, February, and March, even though they didn't put in a day's work.

Feuerstein had other choices. The company's fire insurance would have paid him more than $300 million. He could have closed the company's doors and retired in comfort. He could also have relocated the mill to a developing country, where many other textile companies had already moved to take advantage of lower labor costs and a more favorable business environment. Many of his local competitors had already left the area.

To Feuerstein, the choice to stay in business in the same location was both an ethical and a business decision. Feuerstein, who often quotes Shakespeare, Scripture, and Hillel, said that his role as a CEO is not only to make a profit but to serve his workers and the community.

Feuerstein said that Jewish values must live in the workplace as well as in the synagogue, because all people—both owners and workers—were created in the image of one God. He said that studying Talmud at Yeshiva University, from which he graduated in 1947, not only taught him Jewish values but also taught him how to think creatively in business.

Feuerstein's response was worth the millions of dollars it cost him. His main clients, including Lands' End, stuck it out with him and waited for production of Polartec and Polarfleece—two proprietary synthetic fabrics for which the company owns patents—to begin anew. The publicity that Feuerstein generated was a boon for business, and his reputation as a demanding but fair businessperson spread.

In 1996, he received the American Jewish Historical Society's Emma Lazarus Award—only the fifth person in the society's 104-year history to be honored. According to the group, he was chosen because his actions "speak to the very best Jewish traditions."

Feuerstein's story is still unfolding. In 2002, he filed for Chapter 11 reorganization because of reduced sales during one of the mildest winters on record and competition from cheap, offshore products. Feuerstein vowed to rebuild his company, and few are betting against him because he has emerged from Chapter 11 before. But even if he does not, think about what he has done for his workers and how it has paid dividends to his community and strengthened people's belief in working hard for a loyal boss. His reputation ensures that if he ever needs labor concessions in any future endeavor, he will get them, and if he needs government assistance, he will likely receive it.

Talmud's other tenets about workplace preservation and, more important, extending charity to needy workers.

This concept is borne out by the Talmudic story of a porter hired to carry a barrel. While moving the barrel, the porter stumbled, and the barrel broke. Some rabbis argued that stumbling was not the same as being negligent, and therefore the porter should not be liable for the barrel and its contents. Others argued that the porter had been negligent (partly because a porter is a professional mover and is not likely to stumble) and that he should pay for the damage. Still others argued that the porter should sign an oath that he was not negligent and that the incident was simply an accident, and then he could not be held liable.

The rabbis concluded their discussion with an unexpected twist, illustrated by the following story.

Rabba bar Bar Hanan hired porters to move a barrel of wine, but as a result of their negligence, the barrel broke. When they failed to pay the damages, Rabba bar Bar Hanan confiscated their cloaks to make sure they appeared in court to answer for their negligence.

The porters went before the Rav* for adjudication. The Rav told him to return the cloaks. Rabba bar Bar Hanan asked, "Is this the law, that I am permitted to seize the porters' property?"[15]

The Rav answered that it was indeed the law, but that he was holding him to a higher law, as noted in Proverbs 2:20, which advises: "That you may walk in the way of good men."

Rabba bar Bar Hanan returned the cloaks to the porters but withheld their wages for the job because it had not been completed. Again they protested to the Rav: "We are poor, we have worked all day, we have nothing to show for our labors and we are hungry. We have not received our wages."

Rav was a title given to scholars at the time, because they could not be officially ordained outside of Palestine with the title *rabbi*. Many famous sages were known solely by the name Rav.

Again, Rabba said to the Rav, "Is this the law, that I must pay the porters even though they broke my wine barrel and didn't finish the job?"

The Rav answered that, strictly speaking, the porters were not entitled to their wages, but, considering their poverty, Rabba should go beyond the letter of the law and pay them so he could stay on "the path of the righteous."

The rabbis commonly concluded that employers should go beyond the technical interpretation of the law and into the realm of piety when dealing with workers. Because workers were often at a financial disadvantage, it behooved employers to give a little more than what was called for by law.

For example, contemporary law in most states in the United States allows an employer to withhold a worker's salary to repay a debt, but garnishment of wages has never been permitted in Talmudic tradition. If a person performed the work, he or she was entitled to the money earned, regardless of other outstanding liens or obligations. Wages should be considered sacrosanct, in keeping with the contract between employer and employee. As you will read later on, the Talmud views all contracts as sacred documents, which are to be honored as holy covenants.

Wages should be considered sacrosanct, in keeping with the contract between employer and employee.

Layoffs

The Talmud's overall lesson to ancient employers was to treat their employees kindly and that doing so need not cut into their profits. Someone could be a fair and righteous manager, the Talmudic rabbis taught, without sacrificing the toughness needed to be competitive.

Too many contemporary managers still believe that treating workers kindly and making profits are opposing ideas.

This is evident in the practice of layoffs. CEOs who institute across-the-board layoffs to boost the bottom line are often applauded for their commitment to profitability and for having a tough veneer. However, wholesale layoffs are proving to be a flawed cost-cutting strategy. Indiscriminate layoffs look only at the cost of labor and not at the value created by the working people involved. Nor do mass layoffs take into account differences in contributions by individual workers.

After a wave of layoffs, the ghost workers left behind often experience survivor sickness. They become angry at management for laying off coworkers who they think didn't deserve to be let go, and they in turn become more cautious, less willing to take the risks necessary for stellar productivity. Thus, the company rarely benefits in the long term. Furthermore, employees who remain after there have been layoffs may be forced to work longer hours to compensate for the staff reduction, so they become more stressed and less productive.

A study by Darrell Rigby, a director at Bain & Co., found that among companies with similar growth rates during the downturn from August 2000 to August 2001, those that didn't downsize consistently outperformed those that did. In addition, shareholders tended to punish companies that used layoffs solely to cut costs and rewarded those that downsized as part of a broader business strategy. "Investors interpret downsizing as a symptom of mismanagement or eroding demand and shun the stock," Rigby wrote in the *Harvard Business Review* (March 2002).

The difference in motivation behind the layoffs is crucial. Nobody blames a CEO who lays people off because a business is failing and the company might go under. Although they're a terrible thing, layoffs under such circumstances are understandable. However, it is not acceptable to lay people off as part of a short-term, cost-cutting strategy, especially during a time in which executive salaries and bonuses remain excessively high. This practice was rampant in the late 1990s and early 2000s, as some CEOs laid workers off to cut costs quickly, raising the stock price upon which their own compensation and bonuses were based.

Perhaps the most important issue concerning layoffs is that managers expect their workers to understand that layoffs are a predictable part of any business downturn, but they also still expect loyalty from them. How likely is that? Not very. Compare this situation to that of the workers in Feuerstein's mill, who continued to receive paychecks even after their facility burned down. They are highly likely to remain loyal and hardworking, even at their next job.

BUYING A SLAVE

"For you may not eat fine bread while he eats coarse bread. You may not drink aged wine while he drinks new wine. You may not sleep on soft bedding while he sleeps on straw. Hence the saying: When a man buys a slave, it is as though he bought himself a master."[1]

This Talmudic passage advises managers to treat their workers as they themselves would like to be treated—in other words, according to the Golden Rule. The suggestion that buying a slave is the same as buying a master shows that managers have an *obligation* to treat workers well. Not only is it a profitable idea and a good way to conduct business, but it's a legal imperative.

[1]Kiddushin, 22a

As the Enron debacle was unfolding in January 2002, the *New York Times* profiled several employees who felt betrayed by the company. Web designer Mark Lindquist lost a $56,000-a-year job and voiced his contempt for upper-level executives who sold their stock for millions of dollars while workers like him were given notice via voice mail.

Lindquist, who has incurred high medical bills for his autistic son, said he was looking for a new job but added, "I don't think I will ever trust another company." This unfortunate imprinting of a worker's negative values resulting from bad experience occurred thousands of times at Enron.

Another egregious example is AT&T's former chairman Robert Allen. Just four months after telling the company's 300,000 employees in 1995 not to worry about media stories alluding to possible layoffs, Allen announced 40,000 job cuts over a three-year period. For his leadership during this transition, Allen was given $6 million in salary and $10 million in stock options, which, ironically, became nearly worthless when the share price dropped. These indiscriminate layoffs have cost the company worker loyalty and productivity, and AT&T has yet to firm up its finances more than seven years after the first round of layoffs. Clearly, the company had to cut costs in the face of increasing competition, especially in its long-distance business, but cutting workers was not the simple solution Allen had anticipated.

Show Respect for Workers

Maimonides said that slave owners had a special obligation to treat their slaves appropriately. Remember that these were not slaves as we understand the word but indentured servants who worked to pay off a debt or square a civil wrong. They toiled side by side with the master and were generally treated humanely. Maimonides specified the way slaves should *not* be treated by the master: "He should not shame his slave by waving his hand in a humiliating manner. He should not talk down to him or shame him. Neither should he shout at him or speak with anger, but instead speak in a gentle voice."[16]

Another way to respect and retain valued employees is to feed their passions. Randi Korn & Associates is a small Alexandria, Virginia, company that evaluates museum programs and exhibitions from the visitor's perspective. The company and its founder, Randi Korn, are widely known, and their clients include the Smithsonian Institution, the New York Botanical Garden, and the Philadelphia Museum of Art.

They are often approached by small museums with limited budgets, such as the Mütter Museum in Philadelphia, which wanted to create an exhibition about medical practices during the Lewis and Clark expedition. The museum had only $5,000 available for the research, which would cover about one-half of the labor costs. Korn took on the project because she wanted to promote responsible museum practice, and she values museums that care about their public—a trait she recognized at the Mütter Museum. Most important, one of Korn's staff members truly loves the uniqueness of the Mütter Museum, which features medical exhibits such as fluid-preserved anatomical and pathological specimens, medical instruments, anatomical and pathological models, memorabilia from famous scientists and physicians, and medical illustrations. "We like to do work for institutions that have their heart in the right place, and as an employer, I like to feed the passions of my employees. The Mütter received a high quality product which we partially subsidized, and we hope they will return to us when they have another project," said Korn.

Taxes: What We Can Learn from the Ancient Hebrews

Although taxes are paid by employers and employees alike, this seems a good place to discuss the issue because taxes play an important role in corporate planning and strategies. The ancient Hebrews had some clever ideas that could be incorporated into today's tax system. They also looked at taxes in a way that might make paying them more palatable.

The ancient Hebrews considered taxes a legal obligation that businesses and individuals must meet. Taxes were justly administered and compliance was nearly universal, a situation that, unfortunately, does not exist today.

Jewish Scripture details a tax structure that included a changing tax rate during the seven-year cycle. To simplify the explanation: The early Hebrews essentially paid a flat tax not higher than 10 percent. The ancient Hebrews advocated the flat tax because compliance increases when taxpayers believe a system is fair to everyone and simple to understand. A flat tax encourages businesses to strive for greater prosperity by not penalizing their success.

> *The ancient Hebrews advocated the flat tax because compliance increases when taxpayers believe a system is fair to everyone and simple to understand. A flat tax encourages businesses to strive for greater prosperity by not penalizing their success.*

During the past several years, there have been instances of U.S. companies moving their headquarters offshore solely to lower or eliminate their taxes. Taxes benefit the local and national community, and not paying them—even through legal means like moving headquarters offshore—is tantamount to stealing from others, according to the Talmud. Failure to pay taxes could cause irreparable harm to the community. Corporations and individuals should lobby legislators for a simpler tax system that would encourage compliance, keeping companies and jobs intact and discouraging companies from moving offshore.

In the meantime, corporations should take the high road—walk in the path of the righteous—and continue to pay their fair share of taxes at home. Although shareholders want their companies to be more profitable, they also prefer to buy shares in companies that go beyond the letter of law.

Summary—Lesson 3

1. Wages must be paid promptly.

2. Employers are obligated to preserve and protect the workplace. It also must be a safe place to work.

3. Never humiliate or berate an employee.

4. Employers must direct their employees closely, letting them know precisely what is expected of them.

5. Employers must not tempt employees into illegal acts with lax administrative controls of money, products, or systems.

6. Local customs for wages and working conditions should always prevail.

7. Benevolent managers attract and retain the most productive workers. Leaders set the example for a company's behavior.

NUMBERED REFERENCES

[1]Bava Metzia, 29b
[2]Avot, 4:1
[3]Bava Kama, 52
[4]Zohar ii, 47a
[5]Talmud Avot de Rabbi Natan, Chap. 23
[6]Midrash, HaGadol 412
[7]Bava Metzia, 33a
[8]Bava Metzia, 107
[9]Avot, 1:14
[10]Sanhedrin, 33

[11]Avot, 3:19
[12]Sabbath, 104a
[13]Bava Metzia, 83a
[14]Ibid.
[15]Taanit, 24a
[16]Mishneh Torah

Giving and Getting a Fair Day's Work

An unfaithful worker is a robber.
—RABBI MEIR[1]

As we've seen, the ancient rabbis outlined the obligations of employers, but employees have obligations as well. Despite the employer's
superior position, workers have rights that can check the employer's
power.

The Right to Leave an Untenable Job

The rabbis described two kinds of workers: day laborers, who hired
themselves out a day or week at a time, and pieceworkers, who hired
themselves out by the job. Our modern equivalents would be salaried
employees and independent contractors.

Day laborers, analogous to modern-day salaried employees, had
the inalienable right of retraction. At any point in their day's work they
could leave the job if the work was too hard, if the boss was being

unreasonable, or for any valid reason, especially unsafe working conditions. During this time in history, however, leaving a job that was unsafe was rare because most workers did not recognize this right to a healthy work environment and they served at the pleasure of bosses. For example, apple pickers legally could stop work if there was a lightning storm, even if the owner ordered them to continue work. A worker was also permitted to quit if the employer changed his job to one that was not within the range of the employee's abilities or skills. This applied especially if the new job was more dangerous or risky and the worker had not been trained to handle it. In this case, the employer would be obligated to pay the worker his regular wages or find him another, more suitable position.

The rabbis believed these rights to be based on the Hebrew scriptural prohibition in Leviticus against being a servant to anyone but God. This right of retraction was intended to prevent people from becoming slaves to their employers rather than paid workers.

The right of retraction was not without consequences, however. Workers could not simply walk off the job without some compensation due to the company. Although the laborer could stop work at any time and the boss could not force him to continue, the boss had the option to sue the worker in court, for damages. Such checks and balances ensured as equal a footing as possible between worker and manager. The right of workers to strike en masse was also protected by the Talmud, but, again, the business owner had the right to sue strikers for damages caused to the company.

How would such a worker be paid? The rabbis considered every possible situation to ensure that the worker would receive a fair deal and the company would not pay for work that was not done. If the worker quit after a half day, he would be paid half his salary. If he quit after a half day but finding a replacement worker would cost the company more, he would be docked that amount. If a replacement worker cost less, then his wage would be adjusted accordingly.

NO WORK TO DO?

What did the rabbis say about workers who finished their work early? Should they be allowed to goof off or go home?

Workers hired for a set time could only be given similar or lighter work to do, a concept akin to present-day union rules. Their employer could not compel them to work elsewhere—for a nearby company, for example—because that would be considered a hardship.

The law surrounding longer-term layoffs becomes more complicated. "If a worker is laid off while his contract is in effect, and he finds a lower paying job, the employer is obligated to make up the difference."[1] If he can't find comparable work at the same pay, the worker can demand an *idle wage* equal to at least half of the regular wage. Interestingly, the rabbis took into account how this idleness could harm certain kinds of workers. For example, teachers might lose their mental edge or carriers might lose their muscle. In these and other special cases, the worker could demand full salary.

Michael S. Perry, executive director of the Jewish Labor Committee, noted in his report *Labor Rights in the Jewish Tradition:* "The requirement that the employer pay an 'idle wage' of 50 to 100 percent of the agreed salary undoubtedly reduced the number of sixth-century 'plant closings,' and limited the ability of employers to immediately impose the burden of reduced business activity on their employees. It also provided an unemployment compensation system that was more generous in benefits than the typical state employment compensation system in the United States today."

[1]Tosefta, Bava Metzia, 7:6

TIME OFF FOR BEREAVEMENT

"If one engages a laborer, and in the middle of the day he learns that a relative has died or has fever—then if he is a time worker, the employer must pay him his wages; if he is a contract worker, the employer must pay him his contract price."[1]

The rabbis were sympathetic to workers who had suffered an illness or death in the family and allowed them a day off with pay. Although many companies today have a similar bereavement policy or allow people to take personal days, the Talmud specifies that this particular situation warrants a paid day off. This idea may not be earth-shattering in our day, but at the time this rule was formulated working conditions were often harsh and employers brutal. Remember that during these ancient times, only Jews or those working for Jews were allowed to have even a Sabbath day off.

[1]Bava Metzia, 77b

THE RIGHT TO FORM UNIONS

Unions existed during the time that the Talmud was being written. Rabbis referred to goldsmiths', silversmiths', bakers', and weavers' unions. These associations were given the right of collective bargaining and the right to set standards of practice for members.

In addition, unions also had the right to strike, but arbitration was always preferred. One of the first recorded strikes in history was discussed by the rabbis. The situation concerned a family that baked ceremonial bread for religious occasions. When they refused to teach their special techniques to others outside the family, they were fired by the Temple.

The Temple elders hired other bakers, but the quality of their work was lacking, and they asked the first bakers to return

to the job. The bakers agreed to come back but demanded double their original fees, and they still refused to reveal their secrets. The rabbis accepted these terms because the bakers had not used the ceremonial bread for their own purposes. The rabbis concluded that the family's only concern in keeping the secret was for the purity and high quality of the product.

However, the rabbis condemned other trade groups that refused to reveal their secrets because they could not convince the rabbis that keeping these secrets fostered exemplary craftsmanship. "The House of Abtinas would not teach others how to prepare incense. Ben Kamtzar would not teach the special craft of writing. Hygros ben Levi would not teach singing, and these groups are dishonorable because of their actions."[1]

In other words, the rabbis felt that it was acceptable for some trade groups to keep secrets but not others, depending on whether keeping the secrets benefited the craft or enabled the worker to maintain an extraordinary level of talent and skill.

Analogous modern practices might be unions that limit the number of newcomers they admit because the work is too complex or requires an extreme skill level. Contemporary unions abuse their power when they limit the number of new workers to keep their collective bargaining position strong, even though less-skilled people could do the work satisfactorily.

[1]Yoma, 38a

No Hangovers or Surfing the 'Net

The Talmudic rabbis expected workers to come to work refreshed and able to do their jobs. Employees were obliged to be not only well rested before coming to work but also well nourished. They were expected not to be drunk, hungover, or otherwise impaired.

One Talmud passage tells the story of a teacher of the Torah who worked at night, plowing his farm with his ox. He was so tired the next day that he couldn't teach his students properly. Working at night was unacceptable to the Talmudic rabbis because it infringed upon his performance of his day job. This was considered the same as stealing from the employer. Maimonides said, "In the same way that an employer is warned not to steal from the labor of the worker, so is the laborer warned not to steal from the work of the employer. He should not waste a moment from now and a moment from then, but is required to be very exacting with himself as to time."[2]

What does the Talmud say about working a second job, or moonlighting? At first blush, it appears to outlaw night jobs. However, at the time the Talmud was composed, people toiled from dawn to dusk, a heavy demand on someone's endurance. Any additional work might be physically unmanageable. Today, few people work such long hours, nor do they engage in such demanding physical labor. Modern rabbis argue that although the Talmudic rabbis prohibited outside work, they did so because it led to fatigued workers and poor job performance. They contend that in today's world, if outside work does not impede performance, then it is permitted. The spirit of the law supersedes the letter of the law.

According to the Talmud, workers are obligated to start work on time, not to waste time at work, and not to leave early unless the employer allows it. Rabbi Meir reminds us that workers must follow an employer's lawful wishes; otherwise, it is the same as stealing, a serious offense. "An unfaithful worker is a robber," he said.

What would the Talmud say about playing computer games or idly surfing the 'Net at work? Many contemporary scholars agree that such activities are clearly opposed to the Talmud's teachings because they take time away from work, which is the same as stealing. On the other hand, some say that for many workers the possibility of finding the next fascinating Web page is too enticing. These contemporary rabbis insist that employers who offer access to the Web's treasures are "placing

NO SECOND JOB IF IT AFFECTS
YOUR REGULAR JOB

"A worker is not permitted to fulfill his own responsibilities by night so that he can hire himself by day. Nor should he starve and thirst himself to feed his family for this constitutes theft of the employer's work."[1]

According to the Talmud, workers are not allowed to engage in any outside work that detracts from their day job. In addition, people are not permitted to come to work weak and tired from not eating or drinking to the point where they cannot give their company a good day's work. This also applies to employees who have stayed out too late and come to work tired.

[1]Tosefta, Bava Metzia, 8:2

BE ON TIME

"A worker must be very punctual in the matter of time."[1]

[1]Mishneh Torah, Laws of Hiring, Chap. 13

stumbling blocks in the path of the blind." They advise employers to restrict access to non-work-related Web pages so as not to place temptation in a worker's path. Indeed, more workplaces are using such restrictive software on their computers.

Don't Take Advantage of Breaks

The ancient rabbis advised workers who were on the clock to say a shortened version of grace at mealtimes as well as recite their daily prayers from wherever they happened to be at work—atop a scaffolding, on a roof, or in a tree. Their belief was that giving the employer an honest day's work took precedence over saying prayers. This is an important point because saying prayers was an integral part of a person's daily routine.

The rabbis told the following story to illustrate their point. During a time of drought, a group of rabbis sent two scholars to visit Abba Hilkiah, the grandson of Honi the Circle Drawer, to ask him to pray for rain. Honi, a renowned rainmaker, would draw a circle and step inside it, vowing not to leave until God made it rain.

The two scholars arrived at Abba Hilkiah's home but didn't find him there. He was in the nearby fields, plowing through the hardened, parched soil. They greeted him, but he didn't acknowledge their presence. As he was leaving the fields after his work was completed, the scholars asked him why he didn't take notice of them, and he answered, "I hired myself out for the day and I was of the opinion that I had no right to take time away from my work."[3] This was particularly ironic, because if his prayers for rain had been answered, it would have made his plowing easier in the coming days.

Punishment for Stealing an Employer's Time

Because they lived in an agrarian economy, the Talmudic rabbis often compared the work of animals to that of people. This is not to say that people were treated like animals, but it is an acknowledgment that the two worked side by side. In fact, the Talmud insists that animals be fed before we ourselves eat, that they be treated with respect and kindness, and that they also receive a Sabbath day on which to rest.

The rabbis discussed the punishment for stealing an ox as opposed to stealing a sheep and likened it to stealing time from an employer. Rabbi Meir said, "Observe how great is the importance attached to labor, for in the case of an ox [stolen and then slaughtered] where the thief interfered with its labor he has to pay five-fold. In the case of a sheep, where he did not disturb it from its labor, he has to pay only four-fold."[4] Rabbi Meir's message is that stealing a working animal, the ox, is a much greater offense than taking the sheep, which doesn't work.

Rabbi Yohannan ben Zakkai added to this discussion: "Observe how great is the importance attached to the dignity of man. In the case of an ox that walks away on its own feet the payment for leading it away is five-fold. In the case of a sheep which was usually carried on the thief's shoulder, only four-fold has to be paid."[5] This can be interpreted in several ways, but many scholars maintain that although the thief's dastardly work was easier in the case of the ox—the ox could walk on its own and didn't need to be carried like the sheep—the fine was nevertheless higher because the ox was taken from its work.

Not-So-Petty Theft

What about theft of supplies, the common practice of taking inexpensive office items such as pens, pencils, and paper clips? The Talmudic rabbis were adamant: There are no petty crimes. A theft is a theft no matter how insignificant the value of the goods. There were no small claims courts in ancient Jewish communities; every theft was considered a serious transgression, and court cases were tried in chronological order rather than by severity of the offense.

Why were there no degrees of theft? Why was stealing something of little value the same as stealing something more expensive? The rabbis did not say that fines or punishment should not be based on the value of goods stolen; they contended only that there should *always* be punishment for stealing, even if the stolen object was something of little worth. "When a man robs his fellow even the value of a *perutah* (an ancient coin worth almost nothing), it is as though he had had his life taken away from him,"[6] Rabbi Yohannan said.

The rabbis viewed stealing as a two-part crime. First, it's a crime against the order of nature that God created. Second, and more important, it's a transgression against another person, who worked to acquire the possession that was stolen. Talmudic traditions are often more concerned with the relationship between people than with the relationship between people and God. Many scholars point to the Ten Commandments to bolster this argument. The first five commandments mention God. The last five do not—they discuss only people's relationships with

THE TEN COMMANDMENTS

This version of the Ten Commandments may differ from some Christian versions mainly in the sequence of the commandments. Following is a shortened Jewish version of the Ten Commandments, from Exodus, Chapter 20.

1. I am the Lord your God who brought you out of Egypt, the house of bondage.

2. You shall have no other gods beside me for I am the Lord.

3. You shall not swear falsely by the name of the Lord your God.

4. Remember the Sabbath day and keep it holy. Six days you shall labor and do all your work, but the seventh day is a Sabbath of the Lord your God and you shall not do any work.

5. Honor your father and mother, that you may long endure on the land which the Lord your God is giving you.

6. You shall not murder.

7. You shall not commit adultery.

8. You shall not steal.

9. You shall not bear false witness against your neighbor.

10. You shall not covet anything that is your neighbor's.

each other. Although the Sixth Commandment—honoring parents—mentions God, it is really concerned with familial relationships. Thus, scholars contend that the commandments focus more on people's obligations to each other rather than their obligations to God.

One final point to consider on the subject of petty theft is the common excuse that everyone else does it. This is no defense, the rabbis noted, because it encourages others to follow in our errant footsteps. Eventually, this attitude becomes the ethical standard. A story is told of a young boy who admonishes a man for walking through his father's field. The man responds that he was only walking on the path that he saw going through the property. The boy replied, "That path was cut by crooks like you."[7]

Job Hunting

The Talmudic way of thinking about job seeking is not always in line with modern-day business practices. When a prospective employee looks for a job, he is expected to put his best foot forward. He may show off his skills, his education, and even his personal contacts in order to get the position. However, it is forbidden to go after a job held by another person unless the employer has already begun—in an overt way—to replace that person. In modern times, this overt action would be posting an ad in the newspaper or something similar. This speaks to the Talmudic prohibition of depriving someone of his livelihood. Work is sacred, and taking it away from someone is considered a dishonorable act.

The Talmudic rabbis would have taken a dim view of today's common practice of initiating exploratory interviews with companies when the worker has no intention of leaving the current position. The worker's motivation may be simple curiosity or a desire to see whether a better job might be offered. Looking for another job without really being interested is prohibited by the Talmud.

A similar prohibition applies to buyers and sellers: "Do not pretend to be interested in a purchase if you do not have the money."[8] The rabbis considered this practice dishonest for two reasons. First, the seller gets his hopes up after spending time and energy talking and negotiating. Second, while he is engaged with the pretend buyer, a true buyer might have been dissuaded from approaching.

In the analogous case of job seekers, an employer may have spent time with a gainfully employed applicant rather than someone who truly needed a job. However, it would certainly be permissible to engage in exploratory discussions if both sides knew this was the case.

Work Close to Home, and Other Words of Wisdom

One day, Rav Abba was talking to his ne'er-do-well son, trying to teach him how to run a business, but the lessons hadn't made an impression. In his frustration, Rav listed a set of simple rules that even his slacker son, Aibu, might be able to heed. These lessons remain valuable today.

Rav said (my explanations are in brackets): "I have labored to teach you the laws, but without success. So come, I will teach you the worldly wisdom: sell your wares while the sand is still on your feet [after buying, sell quickly]. Everything you sell you may regret [because the price may go up]. Except wine, which you may sell without regret [it could turn sour if you wait too long]. Drop the money into your purse, then open your sack [receive payment first]. Once the dates are in your bag, run to the brewery [you can brew beer from dates, but get them to the brewery before you eat them all]."

His next and last piece of basic advice speaks to today's workers who must make long commutes to their jobs: "Better a kav from the ground [close to home], than a kor from the roof [far away]." (A kav was an ancient measurement, equivalent in volume to about 24 eggs, which was about 1/200 of a kor.) This admonishes us that a long commute may not be the best solution, and that working close to home, even if it means making less money, might be preferable.

With commuting times on the increase—the average American worker now has a 1½-hour round-trip to his or her job—most workers would be better off settling for the kav, the lower-paying job, instead of the kor, if it meant that the job was closer to home.

Summary—Lesson Four

1. Employees may not engage in any activity outside their regular work that will impair their at-work performance.

2. Employees must work a full workday.

3. There is no such thing as a minor theft (e.g., taking inexpensive office supplies) from a company.

4. An individual should not seek a new job or engage in interviews unless he or she is truly interested in changing positions. A person may not take a job from someone else.

5. Work close to home, even if it means taking a lower-paying job.

NUMBERED REFERENCES

[1]Bava Metzia, 78a
[2]Mishneh Torah, Law of Hiring, Chap. 13
[3]Taanit, 23a, b
[4]Bava Kama, 79b
[5]Ibid.
[6]Bava Kama, 119a
[7]Eruvin, 53b
[8]Bava Metzia, 79b

The Bonding of Corporate Profits and Ethics

He who earns his money from trade in reeds and jars will never see a sign of blessing.
—RAV ASHI[1]

The Talmudic rabbis were obsessed with honest dealings, how a company and its workers conduct themselves in day-to-day business. Today, we might call this overall behavior *corporate governance*, a term that can be defined in several different ways.

One popular definition of corporate governance comes from World Bank president J. Wolfensohn: "Corporate governance is about promoting corporate fairness, transparency and accountability." The term can also be defined as "the relationship of a company to its shareholders or, more broadly, as its relationship to society," according to a 1977 *Financial Times* article.

The ancient rabbis' definition of corporate governance went a step further, to include profitability—provided that profits were gained by increasing the community's prosperity through economically honest and just transactions.

The Foundation of Business

In their quest to explore and explain how businesses should conduct honest and just transactions, the Talmudic rabbis studied in depth the relationship between buyers and sellers because it is the basic building block of commerce. Sellers provide goods and services with a goal of making profits; buyers consume goods and services with an eye toward getting the best value for their money.

At the center of any honest transaction is the notion that buyer and seller be *well informed* and that they *understand* every detail of the deal. If these criteria were met, the transaction was considered fair and just.

We can learn a lot about our own business transactions by understanding how the rabbis parsed the terms of ancient business dealings, because the basic activities are exactly the same. Despite the greater complexity in today's business world, all deals can be reduced to the fundamental motivations and behavior of buyer and seller.

Fixing the Right Price

The Talmudic rabbis considered profits to be a natural result of business transactions, which were earned when people were willing to take risks. Nevertheless, the rabbis were cognizant of the opportunities for profiteering and considered this a serious offense. In agrarian times, farmers and landowners would try to maximize their profits, as they should, but the rabbis prevented profiteering by setting maximum margins of one-sixth on necessities such as wine, oils, and flour. They also prohibited hoarding of these items to prevent artificial price hikes due to orchestrated shortages.

Of course, this one-sixth cap on profits does not apply precisely to our modern markets, but the importance that the Talmudic rabbis placed on price caps for necessities remains intact. Economists know that a free market does not always ensure that the price of necessities

NO PROFITEERING ON NECESSITIES

"When a man profits, he should not profit more than one-sixth above his cost."[1]

The ancient rabbis were very much on guard for profiteering in necessary commodities such as flour, oils, meat, and wine. They set a profit margin of one-sixth for these and other staples to prevent farmers and others from stockpiling, causing shortages, then taking advantage of consumers. However, the rabbis let the market set the price for nonnecessities.

Like food, medical care could be profiteered. Rabbis knew that some doctors took advantage of sick people, but there was not much they could do about it because most transactions occurred in the privacy of people's homes rather than in an open marketplace where prices could be monitored. Many contemporary scholars believe that the ancient rabbis included vast amounts of medical information in the Talmud to provide competition and force physicians to lower their fees. The Talmud's pages include a large amount of general and specific health advice, remedies, herbal treatments, and information on diseases and their cures, much of which can be administered by the patient and not exclusively by a doctor.

[1]Bava Metzia, 40b

will remain reasonable, and government intervention sometimes becomes necessary to keep markets in line and to restrain those who upset the balance. In ancient times as today, the courts and other authorities, such as the rabbis, were often asked to intervene in price-fixing and profiteering cases.

A case in point is the U.S. Department of Justice investigation of price-fixing by commodities dealer Archer Daniels Midland (ADM) during the 1990s. ADM is one of the world's largest companies and *the* largest commodities dealer, with annual sales exceeding $13 billion. In 1996, company officials were convicted of conspiring to rig the price of citric acid, which can be found in everything from soft drinks and cereals to cosmetics and the chemical lysine, a livestock feed additive. ADM's illegal activities resulted in a fine of more than $100 million and $90 million to settle civil suits.

The Department of Justice said that feed companies and large poultry and swine producers—and, ultimately, farmers—paid millions more than they should have to buy the lysine additive. Also, the Justice Department said that manufacturers of soft drinks, processed foods, detergents, and other products likewise paid millions more to buy the citric acid additive, which resulted in higher prices for consumers.

"These fines should signal to corporations throughout the world that they had better take a hard look at their own behavior. This $100 million penalty—the largest ever criminal antitrust fine—should put price fixers around the world on alert, if you engage in criminal collusive behavior, you will pay a high price for your illegal actions," said Joel I. Klein, acting assistant attorney general in charge of the Antitrust Division, who announced the guilty pleas by ADM officials. "This $100 million criminal fine should send a message to the entire world," said Attorney General (at the time) Janet Reno. "If you engage in collusive behavior that robs U.S. consumers, there will be vigorous investigation and tough, tough penalties."

The Justice Department understood that this case was not just about one company defrauding a few others, but that it had far-reaching effects. The rabbis understood this concept too, which is why they came down so heavily against these practices.

Another factor in profiteering was the role of middlemen, whom the rabbis had little regard for when it came to handling necessities. They saw the use of middlemen as a way to raise prices without adding value to a product. In the case of wines, oils, and flour—the necessities—

merchants were required to sell directly to consumers. For other products, the use of middlemen was permitted, but reluctantly. The rabbis believed that if these operators raised prices unfairly, market forces would drive them back into line. If not, the rabbis would step in, much the way contemporary government agencies intercede.

The rabbis had a simple way to determine price for everything but necessities: They allowed the market to set it. Rabbi Akiva said that the existing price was, by definition, at equilibrium and therefore was a fair price. If the seller asked for more money, the consumer would not buy. If the consumer demanded a lower price, the buyer would refuse to sell. Each side had the same power in the transaction, provided that competition existed.

Although Japan has been mired in a years-long recession, its consumer electronics business is still efficient, growing, and profitable. Much of Japan's strength lies in its pricing model, which may be the most important reason for the prominent position of Japanese consumer electronics goods in the world market.

Typically, U.S. companies would design a product, then calculate the cost to produce it. If the production price was too high, the company would either send it back for redesign, decide not to produce it at all, or accept a lower profit margin. Japanese companies, on the other hand, start with a target price in mind—based on what they believe consumers will accept—then design and engineer the product to fit that price point. Japanese manufacturers employ the Talmudic way of setting prices for consumer goods, and this method has worked to their advantage, as Japanese success in consumer electronics products has been the envy of the world.

Although market forces usually keep prices in line, it still takes a strong person to resist the temptation to raise prices and take advantage of others, as the following story shows.

One day, Rabbi Safra was saying his morning prayers, when a man walked by who was interested in buying the rabbi's donkey. Not wanting to interrupt his prayers, Safra ignored the man's inquiries. Each time the man asked about the donkey, the rabbi ignored him. The man interpreted the rabbi's silence to mean that the offering price was too low, so the man kept increasing his offer. Finally, when the rabbi finished praying, he said to the man, "I decided to sell my donkey to you for the first price you offered, but I didn't want to interrupt my prayers to do business. You may have it for the first price; I won't accept a higher offer."[2]

The moral of this story is that reputable businesspeople take advantage of a situation only when it is real, not when it is falsely manufactured.

Giving Good Weight

The ancient rabbis believed that using accurate weights and measures was a crucial part of righteous business dealings. Because they lived in an agrarian society, the weighing and measuring of foodstuffs played a major role in everyday business transactions, and a merchant's honesty and integrity were often judged by how carefully he maintained his weights and measures and how accurately he used them.

The values these merchants transmitted through their excruciating attention to detail in storing and using their measuring devices offers lessons for contemporary businesspeople. For the ancient rabbis, it was literally about weights and measures. For us, it's about being honest down to the smallest detail.

For example, the rabbis were so concerned about the possibility of cheating that they forbade merchants to possess weights that might not be accurate. People couldn't even keep them in their houses, because the temptation to bring them to the shop might be too great. Unlike today, when every local or state government has inspectors to validate and seal scales to prevent tampering with their accuracy, there were no government regulations in Talmudic times. Each merchant was trusted to make sure his weights and measures were accurate.

The Talmud describes in great detail how dry foods and liquids were to be measured and how often measuring cups and weights were to be cleaned. It even includes sections on how to control the froth on liquids to avoid shortchanging customers.

THE CHAMBER POT PLOY THWARTED

"A man is forbidden to keep in his house a measuring vessel smaller or larger than the standard measure even if it is to be used as a chamber pot."[1]

The rabbis probably heard every possible excuse in regard to cheating, which is why they mention the chamber pot. Dishonest merchants would often keep an illegal measuring bowl in their house, and if an official questioned them about it they would claim it was being used as a chamber pot. So the rabbis took away that excuse.

[1]Bava Metzia, 61b

Using false weights was such an abomination that the rabbis considered it worse than adultery. Although sexual immorality was regarded as a terrible act, its effect was generally restricted to a small circle of people, and a person could ask forgiveness, make amends, and offer restitution. When a merchant cheated customers in the marketplace, it was virtually impossible to make restitution because of the large number of people involved. Cheating with weights and measures was a community-wide transgression that affected many people, most of whom the cheater did not know personally.

So it is today. When a multinational company like ADM commits an indiscretion, its impact might be felt all over the planet.

Even the Impression of Impropriety Should Be Avoided

Cheating is unethical, according to the Talmud. However, even giving the *impression* of dishonesty is to be avoided. As in many other instances, the rabbis were not only concerned about dishonest acts in themselves, but were also concerned about creating the impression of impropriety.

The rabbis understood that even a hint of scandal could ruin a business, put people out of work, and result in a lower community tax base. It was bad enough when a dishonest merchant went bust, but it would be even worse if an honest company went under unjustifiably because of rumor and innuendo.

The rabbis offer advice to prevent a company from falling prey to negative insinuations. "He who earns his money from trade in reeds and jars will never see a sign of blessing," the Talmud tells us. To contemporary ears this sounds like nonsense, but further study reveals its insight. Reeds, used for weaving rugs and baskets, are tall but hollow. Jars, used to hold items, are wide but empty. The appearance of both is deceptive—they seem to contain more than they actually do. When a buyer takes his purchases home and lays them out, he sees a lot of empty space that he hadn't expected. He might conclude that he had been cheated—even though he hadn't.

Be open and honest about what you are selling and how much it costs. Never allow a hint of impropriety to enter business dealings. Make sure that prospective buyers know exactly what they are buying and are not led astray by the outward appearance. We've all seen this disclaimer on cereal boxes: "Contents may have settled during shipment. This product is sold by weight, not volume." In the early days of prepared breakfast cereals, consumers complained that the boxes weren't full; they thought they were being cheated. By adding the disclaimer to the boxes, the manufacturers were making sure that consumers understood they were getting what they paid for, even though the contents didn't seem to fill the box.

Be open and honest about what you are selling and how much it costs. Never allow a hint of impropriety to enter business dealings. Make sure that prospective buyers know exactly what they are buying and are not led astray by the outward appearance.

Johnson & Johnson provides a more dramatic example of a business avoiding the appearance of wrongdoing. In 1982, someone put cyanide in some Tylenol capsules that were already on store shelves. The company could have reacted by hunkering down, insisting that it wasn't their fault, and claiming that the remaining capsules were safe. However, Johnson & Johnson decided to take *all* Tylenol capsules off store shelves and compensate the retailers for their loss. The company wanted to eradicate any hint of impropriety by ensuring the safety and reliability of their product, even though it had been tainted by an outside party.

This decision cost the company millions of dollars, because Tylenol was the company's single largest moneymaker. At the time of the incident, Johnson & Johnson's share of the analgesic market dropped from 37 percent to 7 percent, and the company's share price dropped 10 percent, a loss of $1.13 billion. The recall alone cost the company $50 million.

Within five months, a new tamperproof Tylenol package was back on store shelves, and the pain reliever had regained 70 percent of its previous market share. Within three years, the product had returned to its original market share.

DON'T BE FOOLED BY IMPRESSIONS

Although the ancient rabbis warned merchants not to fool prospective buyers with products that looked better than they were, companies should be aware of fooling themselves with situations that appear better than they are.

A modern example is the lighter-than-truckload (LTL) business, including companies such as Schneider, Yellow, and Roadway Express. These carriers pick up loads at various manufacturers and drop them off at many different points. They charge by weight, not volume, and this has become their downfall because modern products like plastic furniture and electronics take up lots of space but are lightweight. Trucks tend to reach capacity before they have much weight in them, a phenomenon referred to as "cubing out before margining up."

These companies thought they were doing well because their trucks were full, but they couldn't see beyond the superficial impression. They didn't take into account that goods had become so much lighter. Many LTL companies have gone out of business in recent years, and others are consolidating at frightening speed. The business is contracting so fast that experts predict only a few large companies will exist in coming years.

Unfortunately, despite the new tamper-resistant container, the same thing happened again in 1986—and J&J responded the same way. Again, the stock price dropped precipitously, costing the company $1 billion in equity. But Johnson & Johnson once again recovered, regaining its lost market share.

What enabled Johnson & Johnson to survive these crises was their decision to wipe out even the slightest hint that their products were tainted. Their honorable responses to these crises are among the reasons J&J has been ranked number one in corporate reputation for the past several years by the Reputation Institute's annual survey.

Undeserved Goodwill

The rabbis also studied another type of false impression, which they described as "underserved goodwill." Undeserved goodwill means that people inaccurately attribute to you something positive, which you fail to correct. This situation is a little trickier to handle because the beneficiary of undeserved goodwill has not necessarily done anything to initiate it—it simply comes his way. Nevertheless, it is unethical to accept undeserved goodwill without correcting the misperception.

The Talmudic rabbis considered it wrong to ask a friend for dinner, knowing that he has another appointment, because it creates the impression that he is really wanted. Likewise, it is wrong to offer someone a ticket to a show if you already know that the person is busy and can't attend. People do such things to demonstrate how generous they are, but the Talmudic rabbis recognized the insincerity and frowned on such practices.

Rabbi Meir said, "A man should not urge his friend to dine with him when he knows that his friend will not do so. He should not offer him gifts when he knows that his friend will not accept them. He should not open casks of wine which are to be sold by the shopkeeper, unless he informs the guest of it. And he should not invite him to anoint himself with oil if the jar is empty."[3]

Rabbi Meir's admonition mentions opening a cask of wine that is to be sold by a shopkeeper. In ancient times, a person honored a guest by opening a wine cask just for him. If the wine wasn't finished within a week or so, it would go sour and be wasted; therefore, this showed the guest that he was valued by his host because he was worth the price of a cask of wine. Rabbi Meir said that it is not acceptable to tell a guest

TRUST GOES JUST SO FAR

"If a customer comes to purchase naphtha the merchant says, 'Here is the gallon measure, please help yourself.' If he comes to purchase perfume, the shopkeeper says, 'Wait, till I measure together with you, so that both you and I may become perfumed.'"[1]

The shopkeeper trusted the customer to measure the naphtha himself because naphtha was cheap. But if the customer desired a more expensive item—such as perfume—then the shopkeeper wanted to keep an eye on the measurements. Instead of saying that he didn't trust the customer, he suggested they measure it together, so both of them could enjoy the scent. Very diplomatic—and practical.

[1]Yoma, 39a

that the wine is just for him if the host has every intention of asking a shopkeeper to dispense the leftover amount into bottles and sell it later.

Our modern mores may allow us to make such symbolic gestures because they hurt no one and serve to make guests feel special; however, the Talmudic rabbis disagreed. A false impression is a false impression. As in so many other ethical dilemmas, there are no degrees of right and wrong.

A modern example of undeserved goodwill is lying on a resume or job application about the college you attended. If you did not graduate or were there for only a short time, you must say so. Otherwise, you may be misleading the prospective employer into thinking that you actually received a diploma from the college. This would constitute undeserved goodwill. It would be especially undeserved if it turned out that the employer had attended the same school, because he might tend to favor your application over those of more qualified candidates.

The Honest Give and Take of Business

According to the Talmudic rabbis, a sale occurred as soon as buyer and seller had a meeting of the minds—that is, when both agreed on price, color, weight, delivery, and other terms. However, there was also a cooling-off period during which either side could rescind the deal.

The buyer was permitted to show the merchandise to a neighbor, a friend, or an "expert" within a reasonable period of time. If this person found the merchandise lacking, the buyer could return it. The ability to return items is a normal business procedure these days, but it was never considered the norm until the Talmudic rabbis codified it for their communities.

NO HONOR AMONG THIEVES

"He who buys from a notorious thief, is not repaid by the owner."[1]

In the Talmudic world of business, money-back guarantees were standard practice as long as both sides were honest. In this instance, the rabbis warn that if you knowingly buy goods from a thief and the stolen goods are returned to the rightful owner by the authorities, you should not receive any compensation for the amount you paid.

This warning was expanded to mean that people should not do business with someone they know to be disreputable, because if the deal goes sour they will have little recourse.

[1]Bava Kama, 115

This "expert" clause was quite important when it came to exchanging money. As people traveled, they used moneychangers to exchange the coins of one jurisdiction for those of another. Entrepreneurs would roam the streets and change money for visitors and out-of-town merchants. Sometimes it was difficult to keep track of the coinage in circulation, as it often changed with a new head of state. Sometimes the old coins were honored, and sometimes they were not. There were also disagreements about the exchange rate, because there were no government entities to set rates.

Moneychangers were notorious for cheating naive out-of-towners. The Talmudic rabbis addressed this situation by insisting that those changing money and accepting unfamiliar coinage be allowed time to verify the money's value. City dwellers were allotted a few hours to find an expert. Those in rural areas were given until the next Sabbath to consult with a currency expert.

This tradition of showing an item to an expert for verification continues. Today's consumers can consult an expert, whether buying a house (a home inspector), gems (a gemologist), or a company (an accounting firm).

The modern-day selling tactic used by stores that promise, "Bring in our competitor's ad, and we will beat the price," likewise has its roots in Talmudic times. If a buyer learned that he had paid too much for an item, he could return it for a refund or renegotiate the price. This idea was contrived by Talmudic scholars.

In the spirit of fairness, sellers in ancient times also had the right to retract a deal if they found they had accidentally underpriced a piece of merchandise. They were given a reasonable amount of time to veto the deal. Today's stores generally don't ask for more money or expect consumers to return goods that were accidentally underpriced. The assumption is that storeowners are experts and don't make errors in which they shortchange themselves. In fact, several Talmudic passages suggest that shopkeepers cannot be victims of cheating because of their assumed superior knowledge compared to others. However, there have been cases where accounting or billing errors have caused utilities, for example, to undercharge. In these cases, customers were expected to pay the difference on subsequent bills.

The rabbis deemed it acceptable to sell an item at a price that deviated from the norm, if both parties to the sale agreed to that price. In such cases, the seller must tell the buyer, for example, "I am selling this product for two hundred even though it is worth only a hundred." If the buyer accepts that offer, then he has no claim against the seller. This works the other way, too. The seller can agree to a lower price and therefore have no claim against the buyer. These transactions were valid only if both parties agreed to them and both had all the information available about the product in advance of the deal. This reaffirms the two basic tenets of any business deal: that both buyer and seller must be well-informed about the product or service and that they agree on a price.

Blemishes and All

While ancient merchants were permitted and encouraged to show their goods in the best possible light, they were not permitted to fail to mention any shortcomings these goods might have. Nor were they allowed to misrepresent an item by neglecting to tell a prospective buyer everything pertinent about the product. This may seem like a fine line these days, but to the Talmudic rabbis these guidelines were quite clear-cut. As Rabbi Judah stated, "One is not permitted to paint animals or utensils so that a buyer will think they are younger and newer."[4] Other rabbis qualified this by saying that it would be acceptable to paint a new utensil to show it in its best light, but painting an old utensil to make it look newer would be deceitful. Again, the issue is one of intent.

The rabbis argued about how far a seller should go in describing a product. One of the most famous stories in the Gemara concerns an argument between Rav and Samuel about a person who sold an ox that was unsuitable for plowing because it had a nasty disposition. The buyer demanded his money back, claiming that he had wanted the ox for plowing, but it kept goring him and his family. The seller said he thought the ox was being bought for slaughter.

IS THIS ETHICAL?

"Traders show the inferior wares first, and then display the best."[1]

The rabbis discussed this practice and decided that it was the norm in most marketplaces. Consumers expected it, so it was acceptable. On the other hand, if a consumer was obviously a greenhorn and didn't know the ways of the marketplace, the rabbis decided that this method of showing wares would be unethical.

This also should serve as a warning for all of us not to agree too quickly to anyone's first offer during negotiations. Just as a merchant may show his inferior wares first, skilled negotiators will put on the table their least desirable offer first.

[1]Tanhuma, Shelah, 6

The rabbis explained that the sale could be voided only if it had been clear to both parties from the start how the ox was to be used. In this case, the dealer sold oxen for both plowing and butchering—and at the same price; therefore, the intended use of the ox wasn't clear to him. If the buyer had gone to a dealer who dealt only in one or the other type of oxen, or if there had been different prices (distinguishing the intended usage immediately), then the deal would have been valid.

Some consumer groups claim that produce from foreign countries should be prominently labeled as such. Supermarkets say this isn't necessary because most consumers don't care where produce is grown. They contend that food from other countries is generally as safe as food grown in the United States and that calling attention to the fact that it was grown elsewhere would only serve to suggest to consumers that it was substandard, when it is not.

The Talmudic rabbis offered an example of this precise problem and how it was resolved. Ancient merchants were permitted to mix produce from various fields, because it was common knowledge that merchants purchased produce from many different fields. However, merchants were not allowed to give the impression that fruits and vegetables came from the same field if they had not.

Do modern-day supermarkets create the impression that all their produce comes from the same field (the United States), or do consumers understand that the produce being sold comes from all over the world? Savvy shoppers know that the only way supermarkets can sell seasonal fruits and vegetables all year round is if they're trucked in from other climates or grown overseas. However, there are many consumers who are not aware of this, and supermarkets and other produce sellers should offer them full disclosure. Only in this way can the sellers be certain that they are not giving a false impression.

Don't Mix Wine and Water—Unless Everyone Else Is Doing It

Ancient marketplaces were full of thieves and villains. One of the most common frauds was to dilute wine with water and sell it as pure wine. The Talmud explains in great detail that merchants were not to water down or blend inferior and superior products and then sell them at superior prices.

There are contemporary instances of this practice. In 1986, Beech-Nut, its president, and its vice president were indicted by a federal grand jury for selling apple juice as 100 percent pure when it was actually a blend of chemicals and sugar water that looked and tasted like apple juice. At the time, Beech-Nut was the world's second-largest manufacturer of baby food. The adulterated juice came from suppliers who were also charged in the conspiracy.

Three days before the trial was to begin, Beech-Nut admitted "corporate guilt" on 215 felony counts. They paid a record $2.18 million in fines and costs and more than $2 million in court and other

FOR GOOD MEASURE

"One may not level with a single quick movement. Leveling in this manner causes loss to the seller and gain to the buyer. Nor may one level very slowly, because this is advantageous to the seller and disadvantageous to the buyer."[1]

In their quest for fair weights and measures, the rabbis noted that some merchants would use a quick flick of a leveler to dole out powder products such as flour from measuring containers. This quick motion after filling the measuring vessel sometimes misses some of the powder on top, which means that the buyer is getting more than the proper amount. In contrast, when leveling is done very slowly the powder remains fluffy, not compacted, and the buyer loses out. The proper leveling technique resides somewhere in between these two extreme motions.

In modern times, we need to be wary of vendors who don't offer appropriate and honest specifications for their products and services or who use nonstandard measurements to make their goods seem better than those of their competition.

[1]Bava Batra, 89a

administrative costs. At that time, it was the largest fine ever paid under the Food, Drug and Cosmetic Act. The suppliers were also found guilty. The loss to the company was massive not just financially but in terms of public reputation and trust. Industry experts estimated that losses due to consumer confidence would top $25 million.

Diluting liquids was not considered a crime by the Talmudic rabbis if it was the local custom to water down wine or any other beverage. They ruled that it was permissible when everyone knew and accepted the practice. It was not permitted for a merchant to sell the watered-down product to *another* merchant, however, because the second

CONFLICTS OF INTEREST

"One may not tell someone to sell a donkey and buy a field when one wishes to buy a donkey and sell a field."[1]

In daily business life we all encounter situations that are potential conflicts of interest. During the past several years, we have seen this played out egregiously by brokerage firms that act not only as brokers but also as investment bankers. Although these bankers promised a so-called Chinese wall between the investment side, composed of analysts who rate and recommend company stocks, and the banking side, which solicits loans for these companies, the wall was nonexistent.

In one instance, New York State Attorney General Elliot Spitzer uncovered a memo in which a Merrill Lynch analyst made highly critical remarks about the management of an Internet business, even calling the company's stock "a piece of junk." However, the company was a big investment banking client of Merrill, so its analysts gave the company its highest stock rating. In early 2003, a bevy of large investment banks, including Citi-Bank, UBS Warburg, and CS First Boston, were negotiating a $1.5 billion settlement concerning similar conflict-of-interest charges brought by Spitzer and various federal agencies, including the Securities and Exchange Commission. Under terms of the settlement with federal regulators, compensation can no longer be tied to investment banking, a condition that is prohibited by Talmudic rules.

It is safe to say that these dishonest acts did more than hurt shareholders who directly owned stocks in certain companies. These charges cast a pall over the integrity of the entire stock market that will linger for years.

[1]Bava Metzia, 75b, et al.

merchant might sell it in a different town where there was not an accepted custom of adding water to wine.

The consideration of local custom seen throughout Talmudic thought cannot be stressed too much. Every industry has accepted practices unique to it that may seem unfair to someone from elsewhere. For example, many restaurants in large cities customarily charge a 15 percent gratuity for parties larger than, say, eight people. Someone from a small town who is unused to the practice might see it as unreasonable, but those who live in areas in which restaurants do this accept the custom without question.

Piercing the Corporate Veil

In 1994, the owners and operators of the *Viking Princess*, a luxury cruise boat, were cited for systematically dumping bilgewater and oil into the ocean. The company paid a half-million-dollar fine, and all shipboard personnel were forced to undergo an extensive and expensive awareness training program. *Viking Princess* officials claimed they didn't know about the illegal practice, even though documents and other evidence indicated they did. They barely escaped going to jail.

Company officials were attempting to hide behind the so-called corporate veil, a make-believe screen that many people think offers company owners, managers, and even some employees the right to deny their culpability if the company is caught engaging in illegal activities.

Modern-day corporations are considered separate legal entities from the individuals who run them. Companies can enter into agreements, form partnerships, and own property. However, companies are *not* entities separate from the people who own and operate them according to the Talmud.

Talmudic tenets subject companies to the same ethical guidelines as individuals. Although the Talmudic rabbis could not have envisioned the advent of Subchapter C companies, it is clear that

Although the Talmudic rabbis could not have envisioned the advent of Subchapter C companies, it is clear that no matter how contrived or convoluted a business arrangement becomes—or how large it is—each person must take personal responsibility for his or her part in the organization's behavior.

no matter how contrived or convoluted a business arrangement becomes—or how large it is—each person must take personal responsibility for his or her part in the organization's behavior.

This message is not simply about punishment; it's also about the rabbis' aim of empowering each person to do the right thing, even if others in the same company do not. As Hillel said, "Where there are no righteous men, strive to be one."[5] And Rabbi Tarfon concurs: "It is not your responsibility to finish the work of perfecting the world, but you are not free to desist from trying."[6]

All of us have an obligation to make everything around us better, and that includes improving the ethical activity of our companies. The rabbis make it clear that we don't have to make a big splash for our efforts to be worthwhile. Everything we do, no matter how small it may seem to us, contributes to the welfare of others. As the Talmud says in different ways (but the idea is always the same): "Whoever destroys a soul, it is considered as if he destroyed an entire world. And whoever saves a life, it is considered as if he saved an entire world."[7] Everything we do—or fail to do—is important.

Honest Advertising

The Talmud insists on a meeting of the minds between buyer and seller for a deal to be consummated. How would the ancient rabbis

BUT IT FELL OFF A TRUCK

"One may not buy wool, milk or kids from shepherds. Nor may one buy trees or fruit from the watchman of orchards. It is permissible to buy from housewives woolen garments in Judea, flaxen garments in the Galil and calves in Sharon. However, even in these cases you may not buy goods if the seller asks that they be hidden."[1]

People are not permitted to buy goods that are suspected to have been stolen, even if they don't have firsthand knowledge of the crime. We are obliged to resist any temptation to buy such goods, and the rabbis put in place rules that went to great lengths to make sure that any suspicion of impropriety was erased.

In this instance, because shepherds were usually hired hands rather than owners of a flock, people were prohibited from buying wool, milk, or animals from them. Under the same reasoning, people were not allowed to buy fruits and vegetables from those who guarded orchards and farms.

The rabbis allowed purchases of homemade products from housewives, which they deemed above suspicion except in the case where the seller told the buyer that the products should be hidden or concealed during the transaction. Some post-Talmudic rabbis in Italy even prohibited buying and selling after dark because the timing of the transaction could encourage or abet suspicious activity. Later rabbis expanded the concept of potentially suspect transactions to include those involving information.

If it takes place in the stock market, we call this activity *insider trading*. For example, takeover king Ivan Boesky received information from a lawyer who had firsthand knowledge of takeover candidates. He sold this information to Boesky, a practice the rabbis would have deemed selling stolen property because the information did not belong to the lawyer—it was not his to sell. Rather, it belonged to the companies involved in the deal. Boesky was convicted and served time for his transgressions.

[1]Bava Kama, Chap. 10, Mishna 9

have coped with transactions prompted by mass advertising, where no such personal connection exists?

When a beer commercial shows beautiful women or buff men in association with their product, do people really believe they will attract desirable members of the opposite sex if they drink that brand of beer? Some people immediately dismiss such advertising, but what about those who are not sophisticated enough to realize that drinking a certain kind of beer will not result in more friends or a better love life? Aren't some people too young or too naive to make the distinction between advertising and real life? The following Talmudic story offers guidance.

Mar Zutra, the son of Rabbi Nahman, was traveling from Sikara to the city of Mahuza. At the same time, Raba and Rabbi Safra were leaving Mahuza for Sikara. When they met outside of town, Mar Zutra assumed that the rabbis were coming to greet and honor him, as was the custom in those days. Mar Zutra told the two rabbis how honored he was that they would greet him in such a manner.

Rabbi Safra didn't tell Mar Zutra the truth—that they were simply traveling to another town. Later, Raba questioned Rabbi Safra, "Why didn't you tell him? Isn't that undeserved goodwill?"[8]

Rabbi Safra replied that Mar Zutra was only fooling himself. The idea that *they* would come out to greet *him* was so outlandish that it wasn't a violation of the principle of undeserved goodwill.

So it is with advertising—and image advertising, in particular. If a commercial is so farfetched that no reasonable person would think it true, then there's no violation of the undeserved goodwill rule. On the other hand, TV commercials can be so subtle that even the most savvy viewers can occasionally be taken in, so this ethical standard can sometimes be breached.

Companies have an obligation to be aware of the effect their advertisements have on consumers and adjust their messages accordingly. Heeding the Talmudic prohibitions on false impressions and undeserved goodwill can pay dividends. One of the most effective commercials in the history of television was an early MCI ad that showed—accurately and correctly—two money meters with their dials moving rapidly as two people talked on the phone. One was labeled AT&T and the other MCI. At the end of the commercial, the two people hung up, and the one who had used MCI had a lower phone bill. The message was simple, to the point, and absolutely clear. The commercial was so successful that it was used for many years with only minor changes. Other companies, including MCI's rivals, have mimicked the concept.

Another good example of effective ads that did not depend on unrealistic images is the Volvo commercials that touted the car's safety features. While other car manufacturers used abstract image advertising, Volvo stuck to the basic safety message, and the cars sold well as a result.

Although the Talmudic rabbis could not have foreseen commercial advertising, they certainly anticipated the phenomenon of tuning out, with which advertisers must now contend. Commercials have become so superficial and outlandish that, according to recent studies, great numbers of viewers automatically disregard the message as false.

A Talmudic story about Rav and his wife demonstrates how this happens. The married couple didn't get along—they were always fighting and nagging each other. If he told her that he wanted lentils for dinner, she would prepare him peas. If he asked for peas, she would cook lentils.

Most wives today would probably tell Rav to cook his own food. However, when their son Hiya grew older, he got the idea to relay his father's instructions in reverse so that Rav would get what he really wanted. This caused Rav to exclaim, "Your mother has improved!" So Hiya revealed to his father what he had done. "I was the one who reversed your orders to her," he said.[9]

Some of the Talmudic scholars applauded Hiya for lying for the sake of domestic harmony (not always a bad idea, the rabbis thought),

THE WORLD'S FIRST ADVERTISEMENT WAS ETHICAL

The Book of Genesis contains the world's first instance of product advertising. In it, the advertiser embellished the presentation to make it more palatable to the consumer, but it was done in an ethical manner.

Brothers Jacob and Esau planned to meet, and Jacob was prepared to offer cattle as a peace offering. Jacob ordered his servants to spread the cattle out so the herd would look larger and make a better impression on Esau. Esau wasn't fooled and did not think the herd was larger than it really was. However, the offering made a strong impression on him, partly because of the fine presentation. There was no instance of undeserved goodwill or false impression here, because both parties understood their roles. Jacob showed his products in the best light, and Esau understood exactly what Jacob did and appreciated his efforts.

It was fair and honest advertising.

but the moral of this story is that lying can become too easy and, once started, it's hard to stop. The rabbis were concerned that it would become ingrained in the culture, just as it has in many modern advertisements. After a while, people can't distinguish between truth and lies.

The bottom line: Honest communication works best to establish lasting relationships with clients and customers. In creating advertising for your products, make sure that it doesn't curry undeserved goodwill or create a false impression.

Sales of Dangerous Goods

Companies are responsible for everything they sell and the damage it may bring. This doesn't mean that a baseball bat maker is liable for someone hitting another person with the bat, but companies should not deliberately make dangerous products or those that can be used for dangerous purposes without adequate restraints and safeguards.

Saturday night specials are a good example. Until several years ago, these guns were legal to manufacture and sell. Gun makers claimed that it wasn't their fault that people used them in armed robberies, because the guns were intended for recreational use. However, it became apparent to lawmakers that these shoddily made, inexpensive guns were perfect for stickups and not much else—they certainly were not suited for recreational use, as claimed.

Then came assault rifles. Again, gun makers claimed it wasn't their fault that people were using these weapons for illegal activities. Critics countered that these weapons didn't have any sporting use—a person couldn't properly hunt with them—and were designed solely to kill people.

The rabbis held all manufacturers absolutely responsible for the ways in which their goods were used, and it was up to each company to do its best to prevent its products from being used illegally or immorally. While the makers of potentially dangerous items had their responsibilities, each middleman in the chain was responsible as well.

In the past, gun makers have successfully been able to fend off lawsuits aimed at the intended use of their product, but that is changing. Prompted by shooting incidents at high schools, the attorneys general of several states are reexamining the culpability of gun makers when their products are used in crimes. Gun makers may one day be held accountable for the misuse of their products, as prescribed by the ancient rabbis.

Know Your Buyer

The rabbis pose this simple question: "Would you give a hot coal to a child?"[10]

The question obviously is rhetorical; its intent is to make clear that a person may not give or sell potentially dangerous items to people who don't have the intellectual ability or maturity to handle them.

According to one Mishnah passage, "One should not sell them bears, lions or anything which may injure the public. One should not join them in building a basilica, a scaffold, a stadium, or a platform."[11] The bears and lions referred to were symbolic of all dangerous products. A basilica was a courtroom used to unfairly prosecute undesirables. A scaffold was an execution stake where people were tied and sometimes tortured. Stadiums were used for blood sport contests pitting wild animals against prisoners and slaves. A platform referred to a gallows.

Although the Talmud prohibits selling dangerous items to anyone who is obviously irresponsible or unstable, the question of whether dangerous products encourage or provoke violence in otherwise stable people continues to be a complex one. Does seeing violent acts on TV and in the movies cause normal kids to act violently even though the movie itself doesn't do any harm?

Psychiatrists studying this problem say that children, especially boys, sometimes can't distinguish make-believe violence from real violence, and they emulate what they see on the screen. The Talmud would compare this situation to giving a child a hot coal. Maimonides noted that if a robber could not buy a weapon, he might not execute a robbery.

The Talmudic rabbis would say that it is up to each game programmer, moviemaker, theater, and TV station to take responsibility for what they offer to the public and accept the consequences if their products are misused.

We've been discussing the negative aspects of knowing your customers, but the rabbis were also cognizant of the need to understand your customers in a positive way. They discussed the importance of understanding what people want to buy, how to approach them, and how to get them coming back for more.

As you'll see in Lesson Eight, on competition, the rabbis were impressed by merchants who offered enticements to customers, such as free samples. They also thought it was wonderfully clever for stores to offer treats to children in the hope of attracting their parents to shop there as well.

Buyers' Honesty

Honesty is not just the burden of sellers. Buyers have responsibilities, too. Although consumers are protected by many Talmudic precepts, they also are obliged to follow rules so as not to cause harm to shopkeepers.

One of the most important rules prohibits customers from showing interest in a product if they have no intention of buying. The Talmudic rabbis reasoned that such behavior created a false impression, and false impressions are always to be avoided. The practical aspect was that it wasted the seller's time when he could have been spending it with a customer who was truly in the market.

This does not mean that people can't window-shop, inquire about the price of goods, or ask for more information about them. In fact, the rabbis always encouraged buyer and seller to build a relationship and understand each other before any deal was made. We still see this type of activity in the Middle East and Asia, where business deals are preceded by relationship building and negotiating far beyond what most Western businesspeople are used to doing.

IT'S OKAY; I MAKE IT UP IN VOLUME

"Buy and sell at no profit and be called a merchant!"[1]

In this quote, the rabbis were being sarcastic about being called a merchant. The sages had a dim view of anyone who ran a business for fun, as a hobby, to boast that they owned a business, or as a way to hobnob with the elite. They also admonished those who ran businesses without showing a profit because of their poor business skills. To the rabbis, companies were run to show profits and do good deeds, and the two purposes were intertwined.

They would have been appalled by the dot-com mania that gripped the world during the late 1990s and the early part of this decade, because many of these Internet start-ups had no logical plan to show a profit within a reasonable amount of time. Indeed, many entrepreneurs were in the game solely for the excitement and self-aggrandizement.

[1]Bava Batra, 90a

However, none of this time should be spent unless the buyer is genuinely interested in buying. The rabbis thought it dishonest to build up a seller's hopes without being truly interested in buying. Feigning interest can be particularly cruel to salespeople who work on commission.

Summary—Lesson Five

1. Profiteering on necessary commodities is not permitted.

2. The right price is determined by the marketplace—consumer and seller. Both sides have the same power to set prices.

3. A business transaction is considered final when both sides have a meeting of the minds and agree on terms.

4. The seller must make sure the consumer knows exactly what he or she is buying.

5. "Caveat emptor" is not an acceptable credo. Merchants can show their products and services in the most flattering manner, and even emphasize their positive attributes, but they must also call attention to any faults.

6. Even honest companies must avoid any possible appearance of impropriety in order to keep their reputations above reproach.

7. All products must have a money-back guarantee.

8. The use of the corporate veil is not acceptable. All managers are responsible for the behavior of their companies. Every employee is responsible for acting ethically.

9. Companies that sell potentially dangerous products (guns, tobacco, chemicals, etc.) must make sure the buyer understands the risks of using the product.

10. Buyers may not show an interest in goods unless they intend to make a purchase.

NUMBERED REFERENCES

[1]Pesachim, 50b
[2]Makkot, 24a
[3]Chullin, 94a
[4]Bava Metzia, 60a
[5]Avot, 2, 6
[6]Avot, 2, 21
[7]Sandhedrin, 37a
[8]Chullin, 49b
[9]Yevamot, 63a
[10]Bava Kama, 56a
[11]Avodah Zarah, 16a–b

Balancing the Environment and Profits

Bits of broken glass should not be scattered on public land where they may cause injury.

—RABBI JUDAH[1]

Because the ancient Hebrews lived in an agrarian society, they were concerned about the land's condition and the best way to manage natural resources. Their interest in keeping the environment healthy had an economic as well as a spiritual foundation.

The idea that everything—including the environment—belongs to God and that one of mankind's jobs is to act as its caretaker plays a large role in how the Talmudic rabbis viewed the world's resources. Not only are we responsible for using the environment wisely in our daily lives, but we are obligated to make sure that future generations have the same opportunity.

This interest in preserving nature for future generations is shown in the story of Honi and the carob tree. (This is the same Honi, the circle drawer, who appeared in a previous story.) Honi saw an old man planting a tree and asked what kind of tree it was. The old man said it was a carob tree, to which Honi exclaimed, "Doesn't that take a long time to bear fruit?"

IN THE BEGINNING . . .

"God said to Adam: 'Everything you see I created for your sake. See to it that you do not spoil and destroy the world for if you do, there will be no one to repair it after you.' "[1]

[1]Ecclesiastes Rabbah 7:13

"Seventy years," the old man said.

"But you won't live to eat the fruit," said Honi.

"No, but my children will," said the old man. "Just as there were carob trees when I came into the world, there will be carob trees for them."

Honi ate some figs and went to sleep. When he awoke he noticed that everything around him was different. He looked for the old man but instead found a young man picking carobs and feeding them to a young girl. The girl's lips dripped with the sweet juices. When Honi explained that he was looking for the old man who had planted the tree, the young man said that it was his grandfather who had planted it 70 years ago. Honi realized that he had slept for 70 years, and upon awakening, he recognized the importance of the old man's words.[2]

One of the hallmarks of Talmudic environmental beliefs is that what someone does in one place can affect someone else no matter how much distance is between them. Air pollution crosses state and country borders, even oceans. We know that dust particles from a volcano in Montserrat can change the weather on the other side of the world. We know that traces of radioactivity from the Chernobyl nuclear plant accident turned up in the milk of cows grazing in Scandinavia. Oceans, once thought to be a limitless dumping ground for wastes, are showing signs of serious pollution. The long-standing practice of getting rid of our wastes by dumping them elsewhere is not scientifically sound and is coming back to haunt us.

The Talmudic rabbis understood the interconnection of everything on the earth. One parable tells of a man clearing stones from his field and placing them on an adjacent public road. A pious man walking by said to him, "Fool! Why are you clearing stones from land which is *not* yours onto land which *is* yours?"

The landowner laughed, thinking the pious man had the ownership situation reversed.

Several years later, the landowner sold the field and was walking down the road. He tripped over the stones, fell and injured himself.

"The pious man was right," he thought, looking up from the ground.[3]

This story has global significance. Companies sometimes assume it is acceptable to pollute large common areas like oceans and the air because they think the impact will be diluted. Individuals wrongly think that throwing just one spent cigarette out a car window or tossing a single piece of paper on the sidewalk will not matter. The Talmudic rabbis asserted that *everything* people do is important. Harm done to the so-called common areas eventually will come back to affect the polluter.

The rabbis went further in their discussion about pollution and the harm it causes. The Mishnah notes: "Bits of broken glass should not be scattered on public land where they may cause injury." The rabbis also considered the liability of the person leaving trash and someone tripping and hurting themselves. Rabbi Judah said, "If it was done intentionally he is liable, but if unintentionally he is exempt." The other rabbis concurred, and this rule of liability applies to all types of pollution.

Don't Take More Than Is Needed

Another tenet of Talmudic environmental thought is the idea that a person may take what he or she needs but not more. Does this mean that people are forbidden to cut down trees to make money? No—making money is a basic need. Furthermore, cutting down trees supplies jobs and increases a region's prosperity. However, it does mean that people should not cut down trees to make more money than is needed and that they must not damage other resources in the process. If clear-cutting a forest is interfering with the soil's ability to keep erosion in check or is destroying an animal's habitat, then the rabbis' position is that we should take operations elsewhere or alter our cutting techniques.

WAR CRIMES

"When you besiege a city you shall not destroy its fruit trees. Man's life depends on the trees of the field."[1]

[1]Deuteronomy 20:19

During wartime, it was customary for ancient armies to cut down trees and use them to knock in the gates of enemy cities. Maimonides commented on Jewish Scripture's prohibition against using a fruit tree as a battering ram if a different tree was available. Even during this time of extreme urgency, soldiers were expected to take into account the need to spare the fruit trees and use another kind of tree for this task. In modern parlance, we might refer to this act of destroying fruit trees during aggression as a "war crime," an act so heinous that it would not be tolerated by any nation.

Waste Not

Not wasting *anything* is another basic message of the Talmud, and it applies to the environment as well other areas of life.

A very observant Jew will not dispose of a pencil when the rubber eraser is used up. Instead, he will continue to use the pencil down to the stub so as not to waste any of it. He may also write on both sides of a sheet of paper because, like the pencil, its original source was a tree, which is a precious resource. This practice has nothing to do with how much the pencil or paper costs; the idea is not to waste the resources given us by God. Unfortunately, throughout history, people have often misunderstood the underlying reason for this frugal behavior and have stereotyped Jews as being miserly or cheap. On the contrary, this frugality is not about money but about spirituality.

EVERY LITTLE BIT HELPS

"It is forbidden to cause the oil in a lamp to burn too quickly, thus wasting fuel."[1]

[1]Sabbath, 67b

During the past decade, companies have begun to understand that producing excessive waste during industrial processes is a symptom of inefficiency. Lowering the volume of waste products is not only environmentally right but profitable.

My friend Joel Makower, editor of the *Green Business Letter* and author of *Beyond the Bottom Line* (Touchstone Books, 1995), notes that companies that mimic nature's processes in the environment are the most efficient and therefore the most profitable. "To be competitive, companies have to be as effective as nature in their industrial processes," asserts Makower. "The forest is the perfect model for companies, because there is no such thing as waste."

In his newsletter, Makower writes: "This is a new world view for

ENVIRONMENTAL LEADERSHIP PAYS OFF

The metals and mining industry is not generally thought of as being environmentally conscious, but studies have shown that companies that pay more attention to environmental issues than their competitors enjoy accumulated returns over 60 percent higher than environmental laggards over a three-year period, and 10 percent higher returns over one year. Total per-share returns on equity and earnings growth were also found to correlate positively with environmental leadership, according to a 2001 report by Innovest Strategic Value Advisors, Inc., of New York.

"We see this relationship between environmental and financial performance in sector after sector, although pinpointing its source is often difficult," said Martin Whittaker, the report's primary author. "What makes the metals and mining industry stand out is the extent to which environmental and social issues influence the bottom line. Expenditures relating to energy consumption, mine closure, waste management, and spill mitigation are becoming increasingly relevant to company profitability. Perhaps more important over the long-term are demand side drivers for environmentally clean products, which are creating new high growth, higher-value-added markets for nickel, aluminum, platinum group metals, magnesium and other metals."

Whittaker noted that the trend toward environmental stewardship is mainly about sustainability. Companies that treat the environment in a friendly way end up having a greater amount of resources for future use and experience fewer regulatory roadblocks to exploiting those resources. "This is an inexorable trend that isn't going away," he said. Strong environmental stewardship is also a way for companies to differentiate themselves from competitors when their product becomes commoditized and prices are relatively equal across the industry. "Companies are looking for ways to differentiate themselves and environmental leadership is one way," Whittaker contends.

most business people, a view that recognizes that while practically no one intends to waste or pollute, it has become a normal and accepted part of business, a portion of the cost of goods sold. As those costs have risen—as the price of polluting has become unacceptable, both in financial and moral terms—some business leaders are acknowledging the need to rethink the way their companies operate, in some cases shifting from a linear view, in which money, materials and other things flow in from one point to another, to a more cyclical view where things operate in loops."

He cites the example of General Motors, in 1991, whose North American assembly plants were determined not to dispose of any packaging material from suppliers. Vendors were told not to use any packaging that wasn't recyclable. For example, instead of using wooden shipping pallets, they were to use corrugated cardboard. Vendors had to eliminate wood corner supports, foam, and other materials that they usually stapled or glued to cardboard boxes.

The results were impressive. Within three years, GM plants were generating an average of 15 pounds of waste per vehicle, a reduction of more than 80 percent. Makower estimated that the company saved more than $6 million annually, with no company investment. Although the company hasn't yet reached the zero trash level, it is getting closer.

Another example is Du Pont, which used new business models, created in conjunction with its customers, to minimize waste and maximize profits. Ford buys paint for its automobiles from Du Pont. In the past, the more paint Du Pont sold to Ford, the more money it made. But because half of the paint sold to Ford never made it onto its cars—it escaped into the atmosphere during the painting process—Ford pushed Du Pont for a better deal.

Now Du Pont is paid by the number of cars painted, with incentives built into the agreement for saving paint. This encourages Du Pont to help Ford find ways to minimize waste. Today, 30 Du Pont employees work full-time on Ford's premises, helping redesign nozzles and spray technologies that have resulted in 99 percent of the paint getting onto cars rather than so much being wasted.

EQUALITY

"Three things are of equal importance: earth, humans and rain."[1]

[1]Midrash, Genesis Rabbah 13:3

Air Pollution

The ancient rabbis were aware of which businesses caused air pollution, and they made sure to keep them away from population centers. This was done for health reasons as well as for aesthetic considerations.

Not only do the following examples show the rabbis' interest in protecting people's health, but they also represent the beginning of what is now called "zoning ordinances," a crucial consideration in business and government planning.

NO SMOKESTACKS IN THE CITY

" 'That no kilns be kept there'—on account of the smoke."[1]

The rabbis did not allow smokestacks in the city of Jerusalem because of the detrimental effects of the smoke. They did not like the smell, but they were also concerned that it would blacken the buildings. This is one among a long list of prohibitions and conditions set for the capital city that were listed in the Talmud. The rabbis had seen other cities damaged by smoke and soot and did not want Jerusalem to become polluted.

[1]Bava Kama, 82b

One Mishnah states that a granary must be located no closer than 50 cubits from the edge of the city. A cubit is anywhere from 17 to 22 inches (the distance along the forearm from the tip of the middle finger to the elbow), so this distance would amount to 70 to 91 feet away. The granary could not be close to any fruit trees or plants because the odors might harm them, too. This was of vital importance because some of the plants were medicinal, and the rabbis didn't want to risk that they would be contaminated by dust from the granary. In addition, Maimonides forbade the establishment of granaries in people's homes, because dust and odors could easily reach neighbors' homes.

This prohibition against nearby polluters was also in force for tanneries and animal carcass storehouses. One rabbi noted that not only should tanneries be a distance of 50 cubits away from communities but they must also be located on the eastern side, as winds rarely came from the east in Babylonia.

UPWIND, PLEASE

"A tannery must not be set up in such a way that the prevailing winds send their unpleasant odor to the town."[1]

[1] Jerusalem Talmud, Bava Batra 2:9

Contemporary scholars argue whether the Talmudic rabbis fully understood the health dangers of dust and pollution or whether they were more concerned about the aesthetic effects of foul air. Although they lacked the knowledge to perform scientific analysis as we do today, many researchers believe the ancient rabbis understood intuitively that when something smelled bad, it was most likely unhealthy as well.

The Talmudic rabbis also prohibited certain businesses from being built next to other businesses. Stables could not be adjacent to wine warehouses because the odor from the stable could permeate the wine barrels. Paint storage was not permitted near bakeries because the paint odors could waft into the flour.

AIR POLLUTION OF A DIFFERENT SORT

"A man should not open a bakery or a dyer's workshop under his neighbor's storehouse, nor a cowshed. The rabbis permitted a bakery or dyer's workshop to be opened under wine, but not a cowshed."[1]

This passage is part of a protracted discussion of what kinds of businesses could be situated adjacent to each other, based on the odors they emitted—whether these odors were toxic or merely unpleasant. Smoke and odors from bakeries and dye shops were not permitted near a cowshed because these smells could harm the livestock. The reverse is also true, in that the smell of the livestock would have a negative effect on the baked goods. Smoke from bakeries and dye shops would not harm wine in casks, so these were permitted near each other—although some rabbis nevertheless complained that smoke could indeed harm wine.

An analogous situation exists in the contemporary shipping industry. It is common for trucking firms that carry food for different shippers to prohibit aromatic foods such as garlic in their trucks because the smell permeates the trucks and has an unpleasant effect on subsequent loads.

[1]Bava Batra, 20b

The rabbis also posed an intriguing question: Should anything happen if nobody complains about a polluter? Is there still a problem if the pollution isn't ostensibly bothering anyone?

Maimonides noted that if someone had a legitimate claim on a polluter, it must be dealt with in the courts. He also noted that even if no one complained, the courts still had an obligation, on behalf of all the inhabitants of a town, to prevent smoke, dust, and odors from fouling the air.

Water Pollution

The Talmudic way of thinking about water and water pollution sometimes differs from current ideas. The rabbis found that if a stream was on an individual's property, the owner of the land was not permitted to pollute or otherwise block the stream because this would infringe on other people's right to use the water.

Current environmental laws in the United States are not that strict. In some cases, landowners are permitted to dam streams that run through their property, and some waste products are permitted to be discharged into waterways. Although modern pollution laws specify permissible levels of discharge, the rabbis did not set any incremental limits. Any pollution that could be detected by the senses (they obviously didn't have electronic detectors) was prohibited.

The rabbis saw water pollution as a threat to a community's health and economic well-being. The Talmud contains many rules that deal with the exact way in which people are to handle their sewage. In particular, they are not to place outhouse toilets too near another person's house, stream, or garden. These concepts make sense to us, but they were not obvious in ancient times. Ancient Jewish communities were some of the first to put such antipollution edicts into formal practice.

Noise Pollution

Many people think of noise pollution as a modern phenomenon, but the rabbis were cognizant of its dangers as well. They did not allow

LANDFILL ETIQUETTE

"The pious ones of old used to hide their thorns and broken glass in the midst of their fields at a depth of three handbreadths [about 11 inches] below the surface so that even a plow could not be hindered by them. Rabbi Sheshet used to throw them in fire. Raba threw them in the Tigris River."[1]

The ancient Hebrews understood the concept of landfills and stated that solid wastes must be buried deep enough so that they would not be uncovered under normal circumstances—for example, by a plow. They also said it was permissible to burn thorns and glass or throw them in the river because neither glass nor thorns would pollute the water.

[1]Bava Kama, 30a

noisy businesses to operate near homes, where they could annoy residents. A millstone was not permitted to be situated adjacent to a neighbor's wall because of the noise and vibration it produced. Recent studies suggest that continual loud noise can cause deafness and may lower the body's resistance to diseases. Contemporary scholars cannot be certain whether the ancient rabbis actually recognized the negative health effects of excessive noise or merely considered it annoying. Either way, the rabbis enacted strict rules against it.

Light

Do people have a right to sunlight? The rabbis thought so.

As with the other forms of pollution, scholars don't know whether the rabbis somehow understood that humans need regular doses of sunlight in order to maintain good health or whether they simply saw sunlight as an aesthetic imperative. Regardless, their insight is

BAD VIBRATIONS

"Millstones should be kept at a distance of three handbreadths from the upper stone which means four from the lower stone. What is the reason for this? Because of the shaking. But was it not taught: millstones fixed on a base must be kept three handbreadths from the casing which means four from the sieve. Now what shaking is there? We must say then that the reason is because of the noise."[1]

This exchange discusses techniques for limiting the vibrations of millstones so as not to disturb neighboring dwellings. One sage, Rashi, noted that a smaller millstone fixed on a base didn't produce much vibration—but his opinion was not universally accepted, and the ruling erred on the side of keeping things quiet.

[1]Bava Batra, 20b

supported by recent research, which has linked good mental and physical health with exposure to sunlight.

The Talmudic rabbis had protracted discussions about how close to another's house a neighbor could build his wall, and they finally settled on about 6 feet. As a forerunner of modern zoning regulations, the Talmud specified that a person could rebuild a wall the way it had previously stood; however, a new wall could not block light from entering a neighbor's window but must be built in such a way as to prevent peeping. The rabbis considered personal privacy a bona fide human need as well.

Environmental Health versus Economic Growth: Which One Wins?

Although the ancient rabbis understood the importance of maintaining the environment, they also were concerned about continued economic

RESIDENTIAL ZONING

"If a person wants to open a shop in the courtyard, his neighbor may stop him because he will be kept awake by the noise of people going in and out of the shop. A man, however, may make articles in the courtyard to take out and sell in the market, and his neighbor cannot prevent him on the ground that he cannot sleep from the noise of the hammer or of the mill-stones or of the children."[1]

The rabbis were ahead of their time on zoning issues as they concerned businesses in residential neighborhoods—which in their day meant a courtyard surrounded by homes. They believed that people should not be allowed to set up businesses in their homes that would disturb neighbors as workers and customers came and went throughout the workday. However, the rabbis often sided with industry over trade and, in one case, they allowed the mill to grind the grain but sell it elsewhere, thus restricting the foot traffic to the neighborhood.

[1]Bava Batra, 20b

prosperity. If a conflict arose between economic growth and the health of the environment, which side were the rabbis on?

The rabbis came down in the middle of this issue, balancing the importance of economic growth with the need to protect the environment for health and aesthetic reasons.

For example, the ancient rabbis believed in maintaining a separation between urban and rural areas. They called for a buffer zone of 1,000 cubits (1,400 to 1,800 feet) around a town, within which it was prohibited to erect buildings or plant trees. This was done to prevent some of the inevitable human-generated pollution from tainting the countryside, but it was also designed to protect the townspeople's view into the countryside.

The Talmudic rabbis were precise in their plan to protect the view, and one Mishnah discussed the trees that could be planted and those that were prohibited. Non-fruit-bearing trees could not be placed within 50 cubits of city limits, while other trees could be planted as close as 25 cubits. The reason for this was that fruit trees are shorter and the branches are not as dense as those of other trees, so they don't obstruct the view as severely.

In modern times, several California cities have unintentionally followed the Talmud's call for a greenbelt around their perimeters. In 1997, San Jose's city council unanimously approved such an urban boundary. City officials hope that the boundary will make the city more livable, maintain its unique nature, and protect the surrounding countryside. According to groups like the Greenbelt Alliance in the San Francisco Bay area, greenbelts help cities to expand in a reasonable and logical fashion because out-of-control land speculation is no longer a factor in development. The buffer zone makes expansion a decision based on need rather than money.

THE IMPORTANCE OF CITY PARKS

"Do not live in a town that doesn't have a green garden."[1]

The rabbis were concerned not only about the esthetic benefits of green space in urban areas, but also about the health gains.

[1] Jerusalem Talmud, Kiddushin 4:12

Jewish laws encouraged the building of smaller, individual towns rather than the expansion of larger cities to serve an ever increasing population. This has become a modern trend as well. Instead of central urban centers, such as Washington, D.C., or Los Angeles, to which people commute from the suburbs, the new model is one of smaller "satellite" cities that are not necessarily dependent on the large center city for their economic well-being.

The nation's capital still draws its share of commuters; however, more and more jobs are being created in the burgeoning Virginia towns of Tyson's Corner, Reston, and Sterling to the east, and in Rockville and Gaithersburg to the north, in Maryland. Because so many people have begun commuting to these cities instead of to Washington, D.C., authorities have changed bus routes and constructed connector roads to accommodate traffic in and around these so-called edge cities.

Rabbi Meir Tamari's book *In the Marketplace,* relates a story concerning the need to balance economic growth against environmental health. Based on the Mishnah that forbids odorous businesses, citizens of Turkish towns in the late eighteenth century complained that vats of dye used for textiles were making life unbearable. The smell was awful, and they wanted the vats removed from the cities.

The local rabbis agreed with them, saying that the law bolstered their position, but getting rid of the vats would throw the town into an economic catastrophe. They ruled that the people would have to pay an ecological price if they wanted to keep their economic base.

Contemporary companies that pollute proffer this same argument. If they close down operations in order to comply with what they consider cumbersome environmental rules, the entire area might be financially ruined. The rabbis would not be pushed into agreeing with this argument in every case, however. If a facility produced pollution that made people ill, Jewish law prohibited its operation. In the case of the dye vats, the smell was unpleasant but not considered unhealthy. (This was before the advent of synthetic dyes, which indeed can be unhealthy.) Talmudic law has always been clear that a person is not permitted to work at a job that might injure himself or others. "For example," writes Tamari, "if coal mining could not be conducted without a definite high risk of black lung disease, a Jewish economy would have to get along with an alternative source of fuel."

Summary—Lesson Six

1. Do not use more materials than necessary.

2. Natural resources may be exploited but not wasted in order to produce profits.

3. Manufacturing processes that produce waste products are inefficient and less profitable. Manufacturing processes should mimic nature's economy.

4. Causing pollution is morally unacceptable.

5. Environmental health must be balanced with economic growth. Neither is more important than the other.

6. There is no such thing as local pollution. Locally produced pollution can have an impact on places and people located far away.

NUMBERED REFERENCES

[1]Bava Kama, 30a
[2]Ta'anit, 23a
[3]Bava Kama, 50b

The Rules of Partnerships, Deals, and Debt

Do not enter into a partnership with a heathen.
—RABBI JUDAH[1]
Eat onions and dwell in the protection of your house.
—RABBI JUDAH BEN RABBI IL'A[2]

If you examine the flurry of mergers that took place in the United States during the 1980s and 1990s—most of which didn't succeed—you'll find that the main reason for the failures was a lack of compatibility, a difference in corporate cultures.

The Talmudic rabbis understood the importance of the right fit when it came to partnerships. Even though they could not have foreseen billion-dollar mergers and acquisitions, they knew better than many of today's deal makers what it takes to make partnerships succeed.

Compatibility of Cultures

The rabbis discussed the dangers of entering into partnerships with those they called "heathens"—people who have no religious beliefs at all or who are idol worshippers. Although partnerships between Jews and heathens were not forbidden by law, they were discouraged because of the clash of cultures that was bound to cause friction. The Talmud states, "One may not enter into a business partnership with a heathen, lest the latter be obliged to take an oath in connection with a business dispute, and he swear by his idol. Don't let such an oath come out of your mouth."

In everyday English, this means that before entering into a partnership, each side must know where the other's beliefs and allegiances lie. Rabbis saw the potential for trouble during a business dispute—the heathen might swear upon his idol in a court of law or before another person. Because Jews are forbidden to worship or swear an oath on an idol, this would put the Jew in a compromising position. Should he support his partner and accept the oath, forsaking his own God in the process, or should he reject his partner's oath and forsake their partnership? The Talmudic rabbis advised that you avoid putting yourself in such a position.

In the environment in which today's businesses operate, prospective partners must make sure that their basic beliefs are compatible. This is something that the management at Quaker Oats mistakenly thought they could overcome when they bought Snapple. Risk-averse companies should not merge with risk takers, and companies that have made a commitment to social responsibility should not merge with companies that are more interested in their own well-being.

Partnerships as a Form of Charity

The Talmud also talks about setting up partnerships as a form of charity. "He who lends money is greater than he who performs charity; and he who forms a partnership is greater than all."[3] Partnering is considered more righteous than outright charity because the recipients aren't made to feel humiliated for taking a handout; on the contrary, they can regard the partnership as a means for the benefactor to make more money or expand the business. Rather than charity, it's a business decision based on sound thinking.

QUAKER OATS AND SNAPPLE:
A CLASSIC MERGER MISMATCH

In 1995, Quaker Oats bought Snapple for $1.7 billion, and many Wall Streeters shook their heads in wonder. How were these two companies—one blue suit, the other tie-dyed T-shirt—going to make it as a team?

Snapple was iconoclastic from the very beginning, building a company from the ground up, establishing a quirky rapport with its customers, and forming a small but dedicated distribution network. The sporty iced-tea seller even had the outrageous Howard Stern promote its flavored teas during the shock jock's early days, when he was building his own audience in New York City.

Enter Quaker Oats, a well-established, rather stately company with beverage icon Gatorade in its stable. Gatorade enjoyed a large distribution network but didn't have the hipness that made Snapple successful. Quaker Oats managers believed they could handle Snapple customers as they did Gatorade customers, and the merger would be larger than the sum of its parts.

Less than 2½ years after the purchase, Quaker Oats sold Snapple for only $300 million, because the two companies were unable to meld their distinct and different cultures. In the process, Quaker lost $1.4 billion.

Charity of this nature also makes the recipients feel as though they have something to offer that others find valuable, and this bolsters their confidence and self-esteem. They will tend to work extra hard at making the business prosper, because they are working not only for themselves and their employees but for another party who believes in their abilities.

NETWORKING PAYS

"A person should try to be a partner of one who is doing well, because everything he touches has a certain blessing to it."[1]

[1]Pesachim, 112a, 113a

If done intelligently, lending money for a partnership should produce a new business venture that might, in turn, lead to hiring more people and result in growing prosperity for the community—always the goal of business, according to the Talmud.

Dividing It Fairly

Because partnerships were such an important part of agrarian life, the ancient rabbis discussed in great detail how they were to be dissolved and the assets meted out. For example, the rabbis discussed dividing herds of livestock that had been bought by one partner and raised by another, paying particular attention to the different levels of care and the range of expenses required for various kinds of livestock. Once an animal had been raised for slaughter, who would do the butchering and who would get which part? The Talmud addresses all of this in precise detail, supported by the cogent reasoning of the rabbis—and they didn't always agree.

These Talmudic stories are especially applicable to today's business environment, in which many high-tech entrepreneurial companies include one partner who supplies the technology in the form of a patent and another partner who brings the financial or organizational acumen. If they split, how much is each partner's contribution worth?

One Talmudic story goes to the heart of how assets traditionally were divided when there was such a dispute. There was a partnership between two Samaritans, quasi-Jews who settled in the northern part of Israel after the exile of the tribes of Israel. Although these people were not really Jewish, they often asked the rabbis for advice because of their wisdom and honesty.[4]

One of the Samaritans was the manager of the partnership, and the other had entered as an investor. The manager decided that he wanted to take his profits, so he counted the money and took half without telling the investor. The investor became angry; he thought the action wasn't fair and sought counsel from Rav Papa, who said that dividing money in that manner was equitable because money is always to be considered as if it had been divided from the beginning. In other words, money doesn't change in value like other assets, and if it did (perhaps due to inflation) the division would still be fair. Rav Papa pointed out that these two men trusted each other, so there was no chance of outright theft, and the money was indeed divided fairly.

The following year, the two partners entered into another joint venture. This time, they bought wine together, but now the investor decided to take *his* half of the profits by dividing up the wine without telling the manager. The manager felt slighted, and he went to the sage for advice, along with the investor.

Rav Papa asked the investor, "Who divided the wine for you? How do we know the division was fair?"

The investor railed against Rav Papa, saying that he was being discriminated against. "Last year you let my partner divide the money without consulting me, but now you won't let me divide the wine by myself."

Rav Papa explained again that money is considered already divided. Unless the partner purposely tried to steal money from you and the coins were not defective, he told the investor, then that division was fair. For wine, the division is not so easy. "Some wine is tasty and other wines are not so tasty," said Rav Papa. In other words, because wine is not uniform and its quality is a matter of opinion, you may not divide it without your partner's consent. He added, "You might inadvertently take the good wine for yourself, and leave the rest for your partner."

Although partners might trust each other, they should not accept the other's word for how much an asset is worth, except in the case of money assets or when there are no subjective opinions involved.

Get It in Writing

Rabbi Ashi, Ravina's teacher, sent him a message on Friday afternoon, asking for a loan as a deposit on a piece of land. Ravina replied to the messenger, "Please prepare the documents and have witnesses."

When Rabbi Ashi arrived, he asked, "Could you not even trust me?"[5]

"You, especially, I could not," answered Ravina. "Your mind is always full of the law and [you] are more likely than someone else to forget the loan."

Ravina did not show any disrespect to his teacher; rather, he honored him by pointing out how much law Rabbi Ashi knew, and that he was always thinking about it to the exclusion of daily business dealings. Nevertheless, Ravina got his point across: He wanted a written contract.

According to the rabbis, contracts between people were to be honored and respected, and part of this process involved having witnesses present during the deal's signing. They believed that the sacred and solemn nature of the event was honored by having people sign the contract in front of others.

Why were contract signings considered spiritual events? A contract initiates an agreement or business deal that will, ideally, lead to profit, prosperity, and opportunities to hire employees and perform other

WITNESSES TO A CONTRACT

"One who loans money without witnesses places a stumbling block before the blind."[1]

"Placing a stumbling block before the blind" is a phrase often used by the rabbis to represent the many different ways in which temptation can be put in front of people. The quote comes directly from Leviticus, in Jewish Scripture. When money is loaned, it is especially important that witnesses be present to watch the contract being signed. Not only do witnesses sanctify the signing of a deal, but they keep both sides honest.

[1]Leviticus 19:14

good deeds with the money. Business activities therefore afford us the chance to serve our colleagues, our families, and our communities. Consequently, the rabbis were excited about the possibilities stemming from any business contract.

The rabbis were also quite practical in their business dealings. Having a signed, written contract as opposed to an oral contract kept the parties out of disputes and made sure that no one would be slighted because they had misunderstood the terms of the deal.

Not only were the Talmudic rabbis sticklers for having written contracts, but they were also vigilant about fraud. Rabbi Abaye offered this advice: "If you must give your signature in a court of law don't sign it at the bottom of the paper, because a stranger might find it and write his name above your signature and say that he has a claim upon you."[6]

Rabbi Abaye spoke from experience. A bridge toll collector once came to him and asked for his signature, saying he wanted it so that he could compare Rabbi Abaye's signature on official passes that he had signed for the other rabbis. These passes allowed them passage without paying a toll.

As the rabbi was preparing to sign the scroll at the top, the toll collector pulled it up so there would be space above the rabbi's name, allowing him to fill in something later—for example, "I owe you 50 shekels," which would then appear to be signed by Rabbi Abaye. While the toll collector was tugging at the scroll, Rabbi Abaye said what rabbis often said about thieves to their faces: "The sages have long anticipated you." This means, "There will always be cheaters like you in this world."

Rabbi Abaye warned people about other common swindles, too. He advised against writing any number from 3 to 10 at the end of a line because an unscrupulous person could add letters in front of it to make it appear to be 30, 40, 50, and so on. (This is possible because Hebrew is written from right to left, and amounts can be written using a mixture of letters and numerals.) Modern consumer watchdogs likewise advise check writers to fill in the entire amount line on the check, leaving no blank space where someone could write in additional numbers and increase the amount the payer would owe.

Rabbi Abaye seems to have been an expert on forgery. He caught a buyer who had changed a deed that read "a third of an orchard" to read "an orchard." Abaye questioned why there was so much space before one of the letters, and the buyer broke down and confessed to the deception.

When Is the Deal Consummated?

One of the issues that businesspeople have always faced is when to consider a deal final. Legally, a deal is consummated when the contract is signed, but the Talmudic rabbis believed a deal was finalized when the people involved agreed on the details, when they had a meeting of the minds.

Rabbi Safra believed in a more stringent test. If it centered on a price, then a deal was done once one side decided in his heart that a price was fixed.

YOUR WORD IS YOUR BOND

Abba was a silk dealer, and he and Rabbi Judah ben Betera reached an agreement about a sale. When Abba came back to him some weeks later, the price of silks had risen, but Abba did not mention it. "Do you want the silks?" he asked.

Knowing that the price should be higher, Rabbi Judah ben Betera answered, "We only had words between us," which was his way of letting Abba off the hook so he could raise his price.

"Do I not trust your word more than money?" said Abba.

"You trusted my word," said the rabbi. "May you raise up a [righteous] son like the prophet Samuel."[1]

[1]Midrash, Samuel 10:3

Today's practices hold that, although two people may agree on a price or other stipulations of a deal, each can legally back out until a written agreement is penned. Common law recognizes oral agreements as binding, but they're almost impossible to verify in court.

Talmudic ethics rise above today's practices, however. For example, it is common practice to make an offer for a company by purchasing its shares. The offer might be, say, $35 a share, which presumably would be higher than the current trading price. Hearing this, another suitor might come along and offer $40 a share. All this is good news for the shareholders, but is it ethical by Talmudic standards? That would depend on whether the target company actively entered into negotiations or just passively watched as the offers were made.

In the world of the Talmud, once two parties had entered into negotiations, it was not considered ethical for another party to barge into the deal with the hope of buying a company or winning a contract.

NEGOTIATING FOR A GOOD CAUSE

"Every dispute that is for a heavenly cause will lead to a permanent result. Every dispute that is not for a heavenly cause will lead to a result that cannot endure."[1]

The rabbis were spirited debaters and enjoyed a good argument, but only if it was for a righteous reason or cause. They suggest that although business negotiations and discussions can be disagreeable at times, if the goal is virtuous, then the outcome will endure. Many of us have attended meetings that ended up as posturing sessions rather than solving a problem or facing a challenge—both of which are righteous reasons for discussion. Nothing positive or lasting ever comes out of these insincere meetings, which are quickly forgotten.

[1]Avot, 5:20

What Is Included in the Deal?

The wording in modern legal contracts often approaches absurdity. Lawyers try to take into account every possible contingency—even outlandish ones. For example, the contract on a house might specify that the shed attached to the house be included in the deal, but how could it not be?

The Talmudic rabbis applied common sense to such arrangements, and saved more time and expense than many contemporary lawyers. The rabbis didn't believe every minute detail had to be spelled out.

In one section of the Talmud, the rabbis talked about what was included in the deal when an item was being sold.[7] They discussed various types of sale—involving oxen, asses, even boats. The goal of this discussion was to reach a consensus on what should be included in these sales contracts without the need to list every individual component. They wanted to be efficient businesspeople and agree on a boilerplate contract that would work well in most situations.

One rabbi contended that when selling an ox, the yoke is automatically included. Another disagreed, saying that the buyer might not be planning to use the ox for plowing and so he won't need the yoke. Then another argued that sellers automatically know what is included by the price. They know what an ox is worth, so if the selling price is higher than that, the yoke must be included. Although the rabbis left the issue of oxen unresolved, they decided, at least, that price could not be a determining factor in what was included in a sale.

They turned to the subject of asses. The rabbis went into hairsplitting detail, as usual, about what was included with such sales. The saddle? The blanket? The ropes? The saddlebags? One student made an interesting point: He said it all hinged on how the ass was presented at the sale. If the ass was shown with the accessories, then the sale included them, unless otherwise specified.

Finally, there was consensus. About a half dozen rabbis agreed that when you sell an object, the deal includes the accessories.

Rabbi Eliezer, perhaps annoyed at the lengthy discussion, said rather sarcastically, "He who sells the building of an olive-press has also sold the beam." The beam is an integral part of the structure. Rabbi Meir added, "He who sells a vineyard has sold the vineyard tools."

The tone of the Mishnah passage seems a bit sarcastic, as well: "He who sold a dunghill has also sold the manure in it. He who sold a cistern has also sold its water. He who sold a beehive has also sold the bees." Perhaps everyone was becoming a little out of sorts about the discussion.

Common sense about the intended use of a product must be the deciding factor for what's included in a sale. This method of doing business can reduce transaction time and cut legal costs.

What If the Price Changes?

Although verbal agreements are not binding by Talmudic law, a person's word of honor *is* binding. The Talmudic rabbis described someone as "lacking in honesty" if they reneged on a promise. To modern ears, the accusation that a person is lacking in honesty doesn't seem harsh, but to the ancient rabbis, calling someone dishonest was one of the worst things you could say.

The Talmudic rabbis did not agree on what should happen if a verbal deal was made but something unexpected happened and the intrinsic price of a product changed drastically. For instance, what would happen if two people agreed on the sale of a company, and the firm came out with poorer-than-expected earnings for that quarter? Since both sides had given their word of honor, would the deal still be valid, even though the value of the property had changed?

This issue is extremely complex, and the rabbis never reached consensus. Some said that a verbal agreement was binding no matter what happened. Others contended that the Talmud's admonition to honor the verbal agreement came into play only when someone had cold feet about the deal. In that case, they were compelled to keep their word because nothing else about the deal had changed. Still others said that, assuming there was no deceit involved (such as the seller knowing that the next-quarter earnings would be lower than expected, but not telling the prospective buyer), the deal should be renegotiated.

The rabbis began the discussion by considering the case of Rabbi Kahana, who had been given money in advance for flax. When the time came for him to deliver the flax, the market price had risen. Kahana didn't know how to handle the situation, so he went to Rav for advice.

Rav told him, "Deliver the goods up to the value of the money you received. As for the rest, it is only a verbal transaction."[8] Rav cited Jewish law, which did not recognize the validity of an oral agreement.

Rabbi Jose, Rabbi Judah's son, took issue with Rav's ruling, saying that a person's word is his bond. The agreement should hold. The rabbis continued telling stories about other commodity dealers who had been hurt when prices had dropped and buyers who had lost money when prices had risen.

In a cynical yet practical admonition, Rabbi Simeon noted, "He who has the money in his hand has the advantage."[9] If the seller had both the money and the product, then he had the upper hand.

The rabbis ruled that verbal agreements were not legally binding (although they might be morally binding); nevertheless, there was a stigma attached to going back on one's word that could hurt the chances of subsequent business deals. The rabbis hoped that those who frequently went back on their word would no longer find anyone to deal with them. This, they believed, would be the market forcing someone who was dishonest into acting honestly.

Although an honest businessperson, Pittsburgh developer Richard Penzer found himself deadlocked in negotiations with the city, in 1995, over the issue of seven parcels of downtown land that he owned and that the city wanted to buy. Some of the land was to be used for a department store that would help revitalize the area.

Penzer and his partners could not agree on whether to sell the land for the approximately $9 million price that had been established informally, without a written contract. One of the issues raised after these initial negotiations was the possibility that Penzer might *not* be one of the primary developers of the land and therefore would not make as much money as he had expected from the deal. Now, Penzer wanted millions of dollars more to compensate him for that loss. His partners felt that it was not ethical to back out of the deal, even though some of the ancillary items had changed over time.

Penzer consulted a Brooklyn, New York, *Bet Din*, a rabbinic court composed of three rabbis, who listened to the case for about three hours, then deliberated for almost an hour. They ruled that while Penzer could legally opt out of the deal, that would violate Talmudic ethics. Penzer, an orthodox Jew, wasn't keen on the ruling, but he agreed to abide by it. "I would have liked to develop or make more money, but you have to go with what's right," he was quoted by the Associated Press.

Are Deposits a Good Business Practice?

The rabbis were wary about the use of deposits as binders for deals. They were concerned that people would be too willing to forfeit the deposit in order to break a deal. To the modern mind this is perfectly fair, but the rabbis were worried that deposits made it too easy for people to be absolved of their moral responsibility to keep their word.

The rabbis did not believe that a deposit changed the spiritual imperative to keep one's word. Money was not the issue; rather, honesty was the issue.

For example, the rabbis ruled that a verbal agreement to give charity was both morally and legally binding because the person receiving the charity would be counting on the gift, constituting what the rabbis called a "state of reliance." The intended recipient would already have made plans for paying bills with the money or would have promised a creditor that he would receive payment soon.

The rabbis maintained that creating a dependence or reliance on an intended gift implies a tacit moral, if not legal, responsibility for the giver to keep his word. For instance, if a person had agreed to a deal—even if the agreement were only verbal—that could save a company from bankruptcy, the moral imperative to proceed with the deal, no matter what else happened, would be paramount.

In today's business world, deposits often are used as an incentive to keep a deal intact, but the deposit money goes beyond being a binder. A company might buy goods or hire workers with the deposit. This creates a state of reliance and makes it imperative that the depositor not surrender his deposit but follow through on the deal as planned.

No Bluffing Allowed

The rabbis emphasized the ethical importance of keeping deals, but were there ethical requirements in negotiations as well?

The Talmudic rabbis were ardent promoters of spirited negotiations, but they prohibited a common business practice used extensively today: bluffing. To them, bluffing was not the same as clever negotiating and could involve lying about the price a person would accept or the terms that would be agreeable. Often bluffing requires the negotiator to say, falsely, that a certain price is not acceptable to the party he represents.

Although negotiators are expected to aim for the best terms possible, bluffing was considered by the rabbis as acting in bad faith. If a person says to his opponent that he will walk away if certain criteria are not met, then that person must be willing to follow through with the threat.

Loans and Interest

In any discussion about partnerships and agreements, the subject of loans and interest naturally arises. In the world of finance, the issue of interest may be Talmudic scholars' greatest challenge, because the Torah expressly forbids the taking of interest for lending money. Yet, without money lending, the world of commerce would cease to exist. People could not build businesses, buy equipment, or develop new products. The Talmudic rabbis wanted to resolve this issue without running afoul of the law, and although their solution may appear as equivocation, it makes

WHAT IS A FAIR COMPROMISE?

Negotiations often require compromise, but when is compromising a fair and just act?

Rabbis argued that a judge who arranges a compromise between litigants is committing a sin, because when a party is right, they should not be forced to change their position. This idea extends to business negotiations in which one side wears down the other side until that side gives in to a compromise. On other occasions, one party might even threaten the other into accepting a compromise.

So the rabbis agreed that a fair compromise is one in which one side concedes that the other side made a valid point and is willing to settle. An unfair compromise is one in which one side gives in as the result of a threat, intimidation, or some other coercion.

perfect sense in the final analysis. Furthermore, the rabbis' criteria for extending loans offer an example for modern lenders that would lower current loan default rates and stem the rising incidence of bankruptcies.

Jewish Scripture is quite specific about the prohibition on charging interest. According to Deuteronomy, "You shall not deduct interest from loans to your countrymen, whether in money or food or anything else. You may deduct interest in loans to foreigners, but not loans to your countrymen." The meaning is quite clear: Jews may lend money to non-Jews and receive interest. This is not an anti-Gentile stance; it simply recognizes that Gentiles are not bound by the Torah's prohibition on interest, nor are they bound by any other law based on the Torah. However, a Jew may not receive interest on a loan from another Jew.

The rabbis did not look upon the prohibition against charging interest as an economic burden, but, rather, as a way to do good deeds by lending money to people who needed it without getting anything in return or causing them more hardship. Over the centuries, Jews turned

BEING DEBT FREE IS BEING FREE OF FEAR

"Eat vegetables and fear no creditors rather than eat duck and hide."[1]

The rabbis made this statement several times in different ways. It calls on companies and individuals not to spend beyond their means. Once in debt, you are always fearful of creditors and the humiliation that being in debt can bring.

[1]Pesachim, 114a

this prohibition against collecting interest into the righteous activity of giving interest-free loans to those in need through Free Loan Societies, some of which still operate today.

The Rabbis Find a Different Way to Think about Debt

To us, *usury* means charging excessive interest rates, but to the rabbis, usury—no matter how small the amount—was considered interest and was forbidden by law. Recognizing that the marketplace required the use of interest in order for commerce to progress, the rabbis devised an ingenious plan to get around the problem of usury.

The rabbis invented *heter iska*, a partnership whereby one party supplies the money and the other supplies the labor. The working partner stipulates that he is being paid for his services and labor and agrees to share any losses. If the enterprise is profitable, the lender is paid a small trustee fee, and the profits are doled out. The money partner is considered not a creditor but an investor.

For the deal to be "kosher," the business must have a reasonable expectation of showing a profit. Indeed, the lender is obligated *not* to lend money to a company or individual if there is little expectation they can ever pay it back. High risk is okay, but frivolous investments

NEITHER A BORROWER NOR A LENDER BE

"All of God's creatures borrow from each other. Day borrows from night and night from day. The moon borrows from the stars and the stars from the moon. The heavens borrow from the earth and the earth from the heavens. Wisdom borrows from understanding and understanding borrows from wisdom. All of God's creations borrow from each other, yet make peace with one another without strife. But when a person borrows from his friend, he seeks to swallow him up with usury and larceny."[1]

This passage explains that borrowing is a normal part of life, but that, at the end of the day, everything is once again in balance without any party showing a profit or advantage. Only human beings lend money to each other and charge interest for it, thus spoiling the divine plan.

[1]Midrash, Exodus Rabbah 31:15

are prohibited. If this simple idea had been followed, the excesses of the dot-com era would never have occurred because the outlandish nature of the ambitions that drove many of the now-defunct Internet-based start-ups would have prohibited investment in the first place.

For example, would banks have lent billions of dollars to Enron if they had considered themselves true investment partners and studied the company's business plan closely? If they had, they might have seen that it had no chance of succeeding on its own merits but would need to rely on chicanery. Indeed, several analysts recognized this early on, but their cries were ignored.

Marc Sternfeld, former executive of Deutsche Bank, gave an address at Brown University in March 2002 titled "What the Talmud Says about Enron." He noted that the role of Enron Chief Financial Officer Andrew Fastow as both a primary investor and a manager in

Enron's partnerships represented self-dealing and a conflict of interest not permitted by Jewish law, although it is allowed by U.S. law. Sternfeld singled out Fastow because he is Jewish. If the tenets of *heter iska* had been applied and true outside investors had been involved, this conflict of interest and temptation to cheat would never have materialized.

Although the creation of *heter iska* may seem like an artificial contrivance for lending money without running afoul of the Torah's prohibition on interest, it is nevertheless a sound way of lending money because it increases the odds that a business will succeed by ensuring that the business plan is sound. It also lowers the risk of nonpayment and bankruptcy by the borrower.

THE RABBI AND THE CREDIT CARD

The most important factor in determining whether a loan should be made is whether the venture is designed to show a profit. Some modern rabbis have determined that the potential profit should be at least twice the amount of the interest for it to be considered a permissible loan transaction, but others are less stringent.

Because this way of thinking helps to keep poor credit risks from acquiring loans that lead them into poverty, this type of loan could be considered ethical and righteous. It's also good for the overall economy, as it limits the number of corporate and personal bankruptcies.

Under the ancient rabbis' scheme, the number of modern credit cards being issued would be vastly curtailed because the majority of purchases made with these cards are not intended to generate a profit but are spent on unnecessary or frivolous items. Studies have shown that the average American family carries $6,000 of unpaid credit card debt and that the number one expenditure of credit was at restaurants.

> *Outside investors must think of themselves as risk-sharing partners, not just moneylenders. This arrangement encourages them to investigate potential investments more fully and then maintain close scrutiny of the venture.*

Debtors' Responsibilities

It is the creditor's responsibility not to extend credit to those who can't handle it ("placing a stumbling block before the blind"), but it is the debtor's responsibility not to take on more debt than he can comfortably afford.

The rabbis warned people not to get into debt at all because they were well aware of the effect of a debt load on a person's self-esteem, confidence, and outlook on life. In the case of companies, high debt with little chance of repayment leads to low employee morale, poor productivity, and eventual failure, which then puts people out of work.

Further understanding of this comes from examining the Hebrew word for interest, *neshekh,* which literally means "bite," as in a snakebite. One Midrash states: "To what may interest be compared? To a man bitten by a snake. He may not be aware of the bite until swelling starts. So, too, like interest, the borrower is not aware of it until it swells up and consumes his body."[10]

Rabbi Judah ben Rabbi Il'a said, "Eat onions and dwell in the protection of your house," meaning that it was better to eat cheap vegetables so you could afford to own a house. Another rabbi said, "He who eats the fat tail [an expensive food] must hide in the loft [from creditors] but he who eats cress [an inexpensive food] may lie by the dunghill of the town [in plain sight of everyone]."[11]

The Talmud is very clear on the subject of the debtor's responsibility: The debtor must pay the debt, even if it means giving up the collateral put against the loan. Borrowing money is tantamount to giving one's word of honor—it's a sacred pledge. Although the Talmudic rabbis stress compassion, they do not excuse debts, and poor people are to be treated exactly as the rich in a court of law.

Studies of companies and consumers have shown that most debts don't spiral out of control as the result of catastrophic occurrences. Certainly people lose jobs unexpectedly and businesses get blindsided by outside forces. For the most part, though, borrowers have ample time to change bad spending habits, devise strategies, and account for economic and social changes that might affect their ability to repay. More often than not, out-of-control debt is the result of inadequate fiscal control, lack of discipline, and poor management.

Pennies on the Dollar

The rabbis believed that some people who were in debt were not always interested in paying off their loans. Sometimes, they were caught in a web of payments they could not meet and then gave up. Other times, they simply decided to ignore the creditor.

A story from post-Talmudic literature addresses this situation. It concerns the rabbi of Porissov, who was hearing the complaint of one of his congregants. "I am drowning in debt, rabbi. What should I do?" the man said. The rabbi advised him to set aside a small portion of every penny he made to pay the debt. "When it's clear to God that you really want to pay off your debt, then you will receive help in doing so."

The rabbi was smart enough to recognize that this man wasn't sincere about paying off his debts and probably was hoping for a pass from his creditors. This is a modern-day problem as well—especially with consumers and corporations that are very quick to make deals with creditors to repay only part of their debt. They may even blackmail creditors into accepting partial payment by threatening bankruptcy.

Although a very common practice these days, repaying only part of a loan is not considered ethical by Talmudic standards. Creditors may decide to forgive debt partially or totally, but this is an act of kindness and not an act of justice. The debtor is still considered to be morally wrong for breaking the contract, no matter what the creditor does.

Creditors may decide to forgive debt partially or totally, but this is an act of kindness and not an act of justice. The debtor is still considered to be morally wrong for breaking the contract, no matter what the creditor does.

Creditors' Responsibilities

Creditors have every right—both legally and morally—to receive money that is owed them, but Talmudic law requires them to act with compassion toward debtors. Creditors are not permitted to embarrass or harass their debtors, or otherwise call attention to the debt. The rabbis believed that owing money was such a humbling and humiliating condition that debtors should be accorded respect and dignity.

Talmudic law states that a creditor may not enter a debtor's house to demand payment and embarrass him in front of his family. The rabbis were even cognizant of the possibility for sexual harassment in this situation. Maimonides said that a man should not take a pledge for a loan from a widow no matter what her financial status, because the man might be tempted to extort her sexually. At the very least, people might gossip about what they believe to have occurred under such circumstances.

The rabbis went further to preserve the dignity of debtors. In ancient times it was customary to pay respect to a social superior first in the street or marketplace. This is analogous to an enlisted person saluting an officer first, to which the officer responds. Rabbi Shimon ben Yohai said that if a borrower met his lender in the street, he was not obliged to acknowledge him first unless this was their usual custom. They should not change their habits based on who held the upper hand financially.

Although such prescribed behavior might seem unnecessary or ridiculous in modern society, it was of great importance to the rabbis. The mere greeting of a debtor by the creditor could be construed as harassment or, at the very least, might function as a reminder of an unpleasant debt, and the rabbis were trying to prevent this by providing an ethical code.

Summary—Lesson Seven

1. Despite overwhelmingly positive factors, if two corporate cultures are not compatible, the merger or partnership between them ultimately will fail.

2. Honor all agreements with precisely written contracts.

3. Money lending must be handled as if both sides were engaged in a business partnership; the loan must be for an activity designed to yield a profit.

4. Bankruptcy is not an honorable way out of debt. All loans must be repaid in full.

5. Lenders may not harass or embarrass debtors.

6. Lenders should not lend money to those with a low expectation of repayment.

NUMBERED REFERENCES

[1]Sanhedrin, 31b
[2]Pesachim, 114a
[3]Sabbath, 63a
[4]Bava Metzia, 49a
[5]Bava Metzia, 75b
[6]Bava Metzia, 168b
[7]Bava Metzia, 78a
[8]Bava Kama, 103a
[9]Bava Metzia, 49a
[10]Tanhuma, Mishpatim, 9
[11]Pesachim, 114a

LESSON EIGHT

Competition Is for True Competitors Only

He performed no evil against his fellow man, namely he began no competitive enterprise or trade where there was no demand for it.
—RABBI HAMNUNA[1]

Competition is a mainstay of capitalism, typically resulting in lower prices, better products, and more efficient service for consumers. Competition keeps companies sharp and focused. But is competition always desirable? According to the ancient rabbis, it depends.

Consider a situation in which a large discount store comes into a small town and drives local mom-and-pop stores out of business. Do the local merchants, who have invested in their community for years, deserve any consideration for their loyal service? Should they be rewarded with zoning ordinances or other rules intended to keep out behemoth companies, or should the marketplace be open to any and all comers?

Let's examine a related issue. An independent merchant sets up a kiosk or cart in the street. Naturally, he doesn't have the same overhead as the established stores on the block. Do neighboring storekeepers have a legitimate grievance against the newcomer?

The Talmudic rabbis pondered such questions, taking into account economic as well as moral implications. Rabbi Huna offered the opinion that if a resident of an alley (comparable to the immediate neighborhood or community) set up a hand mill, and another resident of the alley wanted to put one next to him, the first had the right to stop him because, as Rabbi Huna put it, "You are interfering with my livelihood."

The other rabbis raised an objection against Rabbi Huna's ruling: "A man may open a shop next to another man's shop or a bath next to another man's bath, and the latter cannot object. The reason is: 'I do what I like on my property, and you do what you like on yours.' "[2]

The argument ensued, with nothing being settled until most of the rabbis agreed that competition merely for competition's sake was *not* a positive thing. They believed that competition should be allowed *only* if it added value to the community. If a community already included several ice cream shops, for instance, adding another one would not be worthwhile unless it served better ice cream or offered more flavors.

An interesting sidelight to this debate was that anyone who wanted to be a teacher would be welcomed no matter what the circumstance. A community could never have enough teachers, and competition among learned people for students was always considered a healthy state of affairs. As Rabbi Joseph put it, "The jealousy of teachers increases wisdom."

Rabbi Hamnuna summed up the rabbis' position by saying that a man would be considered righteous if "he performed no evil against his fellow man, namely he began no competitive enterprise or trade where there was no demand for it." This point of view does not fit anywhere in modern economic dogma. It is neither socialist, which would favor the interests of the community and its citizens at the expense of economic growth if necessary, nor capitalist, which would favor free enterprise in all cases. However, it *is* uniquely Talmudic in that it balances the needs and rights of the community against the freedom to do business wherever you choose.

The dilemma can be posed this way: On one side is the right of an entrepreneur to open a business that competes with an existing enterprise and has the potential to put that company out of business. On the other side is the ethical and moral obligation to provide the community, and society as a whole, with better prices and a greater range of choices through increased competition.

The rabbis never reached agreement on some of the finer points of this debate; however, they did come to a general conclusion: Competition is worthwhile *only* if the community and consumers are better for it. Competition for its own sake or to *deliberately* injure another business is not permitted.

Competition is worthwhile only if the community and consumers are better for it.

Let's explore some specific examples.

The Out-of-Towners

The rabbis specifically discussed the issue of competitors from out of town. Should they be permitted to compete with local companies?

Rabbi Huna, the son of Rabbi Joshua, said, "It is quite clear to me that the resident of one town cannot prevent the resident of another town from setting up a shop in a neighboring town if he pays taxes to that town."[3] A responsum offered by Rabbi Abraham ben Moses di Boton in the sixteenth-century Greek city of Salonika brought up the case of local tailors who complained about an out-of-town tailor setting up his shop. They argued that the tailor worked longer hours than they and charged lower prices, and that this was unfair competition, even though he was paying his fair share of taxes. The rabbi ruled that the local craftsmen didn't have a legitimate claim because the new tailor was paying his taxes *and* he offered a benefit to consumers—lower prices.

IS BEING FIRST ALWAYS BEST?

Companies usually strive to reach the market first with their products or service, but is this always the best strategy?

Nearly half—47 percent, to be exact—of market pioneers went bust, according to Professors Gerard Tellis, of USC's School of Business Administration, and Peter Golder, of NYU's Stern School of Business. It's even worse when you drill down into the statistics. Studying 50 consumer product categories showed that first-to-market survivors accounted for only 10 percent of sales in their categories and led in only 11 percent of those categories.

On the other hand, what the researchers termed "early leaders"—those that came into the market early, but not at the very beginning—found greater success. On average, after 13 years they had minimal market failures and clocked a market share three times that of the pioneers.

The Talmudic rabbis were prescient about this phenomenon and recommended to all merchants: "take your herbs to herbtown"—a call to first take their goods where everyone else was selling them. They argued that it was better to be last than first, because the other merchants would already have established a market for your product and would be drawing customers. If your herbs were of better quality or they were priced lower, you could ethically win over some of their customers.

Modern examples bear this out. Although many people don't remember, Apple was not the first personal computer; the original was produced by Micro Instrumentation and Telemet Systems (MITS). Most of us think of Procter & Gamble's Pampers as the pioneer in disposable diapers, but it was actually Johnson & Johnson that sold the first disposable diapers in 1935 under the name Chux.

Tellis and Golder's 1996 report, "First to Market, First to Fail? Real Causes of Enduring Market Leadership," notes that

being first and alone in the field sometimes means that there is no market for your product. They add that it's quite common for pioneers to have great ideas but poor execution and follow-through. Followers often take the pioneer's breakthrough idea but apply better management, marketing, distribution, and capital to it.

The tax parity issue was key to the rabbis' decision. A similar problem has arisen recently in New York, Washington, D.C., and other cities where sidewalk vendors were selling items at prices lower than those in surrounding stores. To level the playing field, these cities now require such vendors to purchase special sidewalk business licenses and collect sales taxes on the merchandise they sell.

This Talmudic principle is regularly violated by communities eager to entice new businesses to locate in their area. It's become customary to offer potential incoming companies tax breaks and similar considerations for opening new facilities in areas that need an economic infusion. Is this fair to existing businesses in the area? Probably not—although this would depend on the severity of the economic conditions in the area and the nature of the existing businesses that might be injured.

Talmudic tradition would consider this to be an issue of justice rather than economics. Writing in the Summer 1994 newsletter of the Center for Business Ethics, Director Meir Tamari noted, "Alternative solutions to the moral problems raised by competition are usually viewed as a balance between efficiency and equity. A Jewish perspective would perhaps rather see the whole issue as a balance between justice and mercy. This is a perspective that has consequences different from the usual academic view."

Does a community have the right to keep out new companies for reasons other than economic? For example, is it ethical to bar a business because it changes the tone of a community or because it strains the area's natural resources or physical infrastructure? It is becoming increasingly necessary to consider such complex issues. When a developer wants to build a community of homes or a shopping mall, the environmental impact as well as the impact on services and the character of the neighborhood should be considered. The Talmudic rabbis believed that communities must take into account all the possible ramifications of allowing an incoming business—not just the economic concerns. They contend that communities have the right to bar companies that would have a negative impact.

The Talmud Takes on Category Killers

An ancient shopkeeper was offering parched corn and nuts to children as treats. His plan was to entice children into the store so their families would do all their food shopping there. This is not so different from McDonald's offering Beanie Babies or Disney-related toys to attract young customers and their parents.

Rabbi Judah was outraged; he considered it unfair competition. However, his ideas were pounced on by the other rabbis, who disagreed with him. As one rabbi explained, "You distribute nuts, and another shopkeeper gives plums."[4]

Rabbi Judah was also angry that the same merchant lowered his prices below those of his fellow shopkeepers. The other rabbis disagreed on this point as well, arguing that this was good for customers and that the shopkeeper should be applauded. Lowering prices was considered a fair method of competition.

So what's a small retailer to do if a huge competitor offers customers free items or a wide selection and lower prices? The rabbis made it clear that out-of-town competitors should offer different products, services, and prices, but so should established stores. The key to survival, the rabbis suggested, was to be different—and better—than the competition.

Category killers are retail stores with a narrow product focus, like toys, consumer electronics, or hardware, but with an unusually wide breadth and depth to that product range. Regardless of competition from these category killers and mammoth discounters, smaller retailers can still prosper and even dominate their geographic market by offering unique merchandise, personalized service, and technical expertise. These are areas in which larger companies do not excel, according to a study conducted by Dun & Bradstreet and G.A. Wright, a Denver consulting firm, which studied large retailers from 1985 through 1993. The report noted that in order to be successful, small retailers must carry the staples of their industry at competitive prices to attract customers, then dazzle them with super service and special products that the giants don't carry.

Small computer retailers are discovering that, because of the technical complexity of their products, customers are attracted by the kind of individualized attention that they can't get at larger chain stores. Customers are generally willing to pay a premium price for computer equipment if they know that they can call a qualified technician at the store when they have problems.

The same principle has proven true for mom-and-pop video stores. Price is not an issue for their clientele, but selection *is*. Small stores prosper when they carry videos that the large stores won't carry. This includes foreign films, art films from independent producers, cult horror classics, and, yes, even adult films.

Monopolies

The rabbis opposed monopolies on the grounds that they are inefficient and don't offer consumers the best price. One story tells of the only two butchers in a town who conspired so that each would sell meat only on specific days. The agreement was so precise that if one of them killed a cow and it wasn't his day to sell, the other one could destroy the meat. It was a case of honor among thieves.

These butchers had failed to get prior approval from the town rabbi for their plan and thus were forced to make restitution to the community. Scholars interpret this to mean that monopolies would be allowed if they were approved by, as a later passage put it, a "distinguished person." The assumption is that the distinguished person, or a governing body, would allow a monopoly if it was in the best interest of the community.[5]

A PARABLE ABOUT COMPETITION

Rabbi Meir of Premishlan, near Lvov in the Ukraine, was one of the leading Chasidic sages of the early nineteenth century. He is featured in this story about the way a person's mind can be clouded by competition that doesn't really exist. The story also addresses the need to have faith in God's abundance.

A follower of the rabbi complained to him about a man who had started a competing business. "He is taking away my livelihood!" he said. "You must tell him to close his shop!"

Rabbi Meir said to the man, "Have you ever noticed how a horse behaves when he is led to a water hole? He begins to paw angrily at the water with his hooves. Only when the water is well-muddied and less tasty does he begin to drink. Why does the horse act this way?"

"I don't know," replied the man.

"Because the horse sees his reflection in the water and thinks that another horse has come to drink his water. So he kicks and paws until he has 'chased away' the other horse. What the horse doesn't understand," said Rabbi Meir, "is that God has created enough water for all the horses."

Natural monopolies that are mandated by governments, such as utility companies, are beneficial if they are able to offer the best service and the best price. Due to recent trends toward deregulation, natural monopolies are rapidly disappearing.

Protection of Intellectual Property

One of a company's most important competitive advantages—sometimes its only advantage—is intellectual property in the form of proprietary processes; copyrighted written, audio, and video material; patents; software; formulas; designs; and trademarks.

The value and protection of intellectual property, including intangibles such as ideas or concepts, were not a trivial matter to the Talmudic rabbis, who first recognized these issues in regard to fishing practices. Fishermen would often put dead fish in their nets to attract a school of other fish. The rabbis recognized this practice—knowing the bait that worked best and spending money for it—as a form of intellectual property, and they deemed this valuable. They ruled that nets had to be kept far from each other so that one fisherman did not reap the benefit of another's know-how or investment in bait fish: "Fishing nets must be kept away from the hiding place of a fish which has been spied by another fisherman."[6]

Jewish law sets a higher standard for intellectual property rights than do most modern laws. For example, according to *Economic Public Policy and Jewish Law,* by Rabbi Aaron Levine, a minimal amount of copying is allowed by U.S. statute for specific educational and scientific purposes; however, Jewish law prohibits copying for any reason. "Our comparison of [Jewish Law] and American law in regard to the issue of unauthorized copying has found that [Jewish Law] goes beyond American law in protecting the property owner against infringement."

PROTECTING A SPECIFIC USE OF
INTELLECTUAL PROPERTY

The owner of any intellectual property obviously wants to make the most money from his efforts so he is allowed to put limits on the use of his property by others. In some cases he may charge a fee, but in other cases he might not. For example, most copyright holders permit nonprofit associations or agencies to copy their material if they don't use it to make money themselves. This distinction of intended use is clear-cut.

Rabbi Meir explains it in Talmudic terms: "If one hires an ass to ride to the top of the mountain, but instead drives it on the plain, or if one hires it to ride to the plain but drives it to the mountain instead and it perishes, the hirer is liable for damages if the ass dies even if both are only for ten miles."[1]

The underlying theme is that the copyright holder does not relinquish any rights when he allows someone to use his property *only* in a very specific manner, but use it nonetheless. Any deviation from this specified manner is not permitted. Using the property for some other purpose—even one that is only slightly different—is unethical. This precept closely tracks our modern laws.

Levine and others contend that U.S. law allows some copying (such as taping a TV show for private use), which makes it more difficult to enforce statutes against unauthorized and blatantly illegal copying. People will often take the position that if a small amount of copying is allowed, then a little more can't do any harm. Copying is often regarded as something that is not strictly and absolutely unlawful, but is a matter of degree. As you've seen, the Talmud does not recognize degrees of theft. The rabbis believed that turning a blind eye would inevitably lead to a gradual acceptance of a practice until it became uncontrollable.

Napster is a good case in point. This Internet-based and now-defunct web site company allowed online trading of recorded songs among music lovers, who often violated copyright laws. The recording industry claimed it lost hundreds of millions of dollars to Napster users before it curtailed its operations through legal means. Similar technology-enabled services have popped up, and it's only a matter of time before pirated feature movies are distributed illegally over the Internet.

The Talmud's lesson on this theme is that companies need to be more swiftly proactive about protecting their intellectual property and preventing small amounts of illegal copying before the floodgates are opened and it's too late to stop the practice.

The Talmud holds that the owner of intellectual property has an absolute right of ownership, and this owner alone should profit from the work and decide its disposition.

Summary—Lesson Eight

1. Do not compete with established companies unless your products and services are substantially different in price, quality, and selection.

2. New competitors must compete on a level playing field with established companies. This means paying the same taxes and comparable wages.

3. Robust competition always benefits consumers.

4. A small company can successfully compete with larger companies by finding an underserved niche.

5. Intellectual property must be vigorously protected in order for companies to prosper.

NUMBERED REFERENCES

[1] Makkot, 24a
[2] Bava Batra, 21b
[3] Ibid.
[4] Ibid.
[5] Bava Batra, 9a
[6] Bava Batra, 21b

Education Is a Lifelong Process

One who does not increase his knowledge, decreases it.
—HILLEL[1]

To the Talmudic rabbis, no question or possibility was off-limits. Unlike many other religions, Judaism permits—even heartily encourages—its practitioners to question God's authority, his actions, and his very existence. The earliest rabbis discussed outlandish speculations for their time, such as what it would be like to live on the moon or travel underwater.

The Talmudic rabbis encouraged this kind of critical, unconventional thinking through lifelong learning and study, activities they believed would result in personal growth and business success.

An Educated Workforce

Although the concept of learning organizations has been around since the 1940s, only in recent years have companies begun to embrace the idea that continuous education is the key to survival during highly competitive times.

DELTA WIRE'S MOST VALUABLE ASSET

When Delta Wire Corporation, maker of steel, tire bead, and fiber-optic support wires, decided in the early 1980s to move its facilities to Clarksdale, Mississippi, it faced a seemingly insurmountable problem. The company was tackling brutal challenges from competitors and increasing customer demands, but its workers in this low-income, rural area were not up to the task because of poor skills and lack of education.

Company president George Walker understood that his company's survival depended on educating its 100 employees, but it took time for Walker to persuade workers that education was necessary. He convinced them that education equaled job security, and he arranged a three-year program through the local community college and Mississippi State University that covered everything from basic reading and math skills to statistical process control.

By the early 1990s, the company not only enjoyed low turnover and 20 percent growth in employment, but received awards for quality from its largest customers, Goodyear and Eveready. At the time, Walker commented to *HR Magazine:* "My biggest company asset now is what is in my employees' minds."

While large companies are in the forefront, small companies, too, are realizing that their most important asset is not bricks, mortar, or machines but a highly educated workforce.

To say that continuous education and training are the key to business success seems almost superfluous these days, but it wasn't so long ago that the majority of companies refused to train workers. Many company CEOs are still loath to accept the obvious fact that continuous learning—instituted by the company—is necessary for survival.

One reason, perhaps, is that many of the nation's CEOs, now in their 50s and 60s, never underwent continuous formal training once they entered their companies. They learned by experience, picking up what they needed to know along the way, in an informal manner.

THE ROI OF TRAINING

A study of 575 U.S.-based public companies during 1996, 1997, and 1998 by the American Society for Training & Development found that firms that invested $680 more in training per employee than the average company in the study improved their total stockholder return the next year by six percentage points, even after considering other factors.

Moreover, those companies in the top half of the survey, which had spent more on training, had an average total stockholder return the following year of 36.9 percent, while those at the bottom of the list, which had spent less, experienced a return of 19.8 percent the following year.

Furthermore, researchers found that firms in the top quarter of the study group—those that had invested $1,595 per employee on training—experienced 24 percent higher gross margins, 218 percent higher income per employee, and 26 percent higher price-to-book ratios than those in the bottom quarter, which had invested an average of $128 per employee.

High-technology industries exploded the myth that people could learn what they needed in college. These industries operate in fast-changing technical environments, and it's become a rule of thumb that what a person learned in college is outmoded in about three or four years. Even Federal Reserve Chairman Alan Greenspan, in a speech given in September 1997 at Kenan-Flagler Business School at the University of North Carolina, noted that "innovations are making education in the business sector a lifelong activity."

One of the difficult issues for management has always been proving that education and training pay off. Like money spent on advertising, the numbers can get slippery very quickly.

However, training does indeed offer a return on investment. An example of training payoff is Land Rover University, established in 1995, which is required of all company employees. The in-house school, with an annual budget between $4 and $5 million, offers classes on management skills, communication skills, and off-the-road driving skills. According to university officials, the company cannot calculate how much the school contributes to the bottom line, but the effect is felt nonetheless. The company doubled its national car sales average, because, officials noted, the university's curriculum is integrated into the company's retail efforts.

Motorola also has been able to validate its educational efforts in dollars and cents. Motorola University has shown that its programs bring in $30 in productivity gains for every $1 spent in training. One of its main programs, the China Accelerated Management Program, or CAMP, supports the company's efforts in the growing Chinese market. The 12-month initiative uses a five-step program that encompasses training, rotation, mentoring, and "action learning" to help develop management skills. As the company enters other markets in Asia, Latin America, and Eastern Europe, the CAMP will serve as an educational model for training and development efforts in those regions.

This notion of lifelong, continuous study is what Hillel meant when he said, "One who does not increase his knowledge, decreases it." A person who doesn't stay open to learning throughout his entire life is doomed to fall behind. Hillel continued the thought: "He who does not study undermines his right to life."

WHO ARE YOUR COMPANY'S PROTECTORS?

Three Palestinian rabbis were sent on a fact-finding mission to assess the state of education throughout the country. They came upon a town that didn't seem to have any teachers, and they said to the townspeople, "Bring us the protectors of your town."

The townspeople brought forth the town's militia.

The rabbis said, "These are not the protectors of your town. These are the destroyers."

"Who, then, are the protectors of our town?" the townspeople asked.

"The teachers," the rabbis answered.[1]

This story illustrates that an educated workforce is a company's best defense against aggressive competitors and the vagaries of the marketplace. While many companies spend much of their resources protecting themselves from outside threats, they would be wiser to strengthen their market positions from within, through increased education of their workforce.

[1]Chagigah, 76c

The Talmud Way of Education: It Shouldn't Be Easy

To Western minds, the Talmud is written in a peculiar fashion. Because of a quirk in punctuation protocol, declarative sentences can legitimately be read as questions; questions often can be read as declarative sentences. Talmudic scholars purposely read the same passage in different ways so they are forced to interpret the text in different ways. There is no one correct way, and this spurs discussion and debate among students.

In addition, fast learning is discouraged. People are encouraged to read material over and over until they see something new. Students are not expected to understand everything the first, second, third, or even the hundredth time. Each time a person studies a Talmud chapter, for example, he learns something different, and he becomes a different person because of it. The oddly named sage Ben Bag Bag said in the Talmud, "Turn the Torah over and turn it over again, for everything is in it. Contemplate it, wax gray and old over it."[2]

ANCIENT LEARNING TECHNIQUES

"A person does not fully understand the Torah until he stumbles over its words."[1]

The Talmudic rabbis advocated a certain kind of learning that can best be described as on-the-job training. They believed that people learn best when they continue to study a topic (in this case, the Torah), chipping away at it and peeling back the layers of understanding slowly and methodically. They believed in learning by doing, making mistakes, and moving on, until you finally figure out the material.

A related Talmudic passage reads: "A person who repeats a chapter a hundred times is not to be compared to a person who repeated it a hundred one times."[2] This means that even though you may think you understand material because you've studied it extensively, there's still more to learn by continuing to probe and examine it.

[1]Gittin, 43a
[2]Chigigah, 9b

In the same way that sages kept turning over the Talmud to find new answers, businesses very often find that the solution to a gnawing business problem is right in front of them if they continue to turn it over.

Coke Finds the Answer

After the accounting scandals in the late 1990s and early 2000s, many public companies felt themselves to be under siege, faced with an angry investing public and analysts who judged every slight move they made. Traditionally, public companies issue estimates of their quarterly results weeks or months in advance. In the climate of the times, they felt pressured to meet those estimates, and in order to do so they started fudging the numbers, at first in small ways. Eventually, the pressure became so intense that these companies started manipulating their numbers in a wholesale fashion.

Coca-Cola's management took a step back to examine how they could avoid this vicious cycle in their company. They considered releasing very conservative figures or releasing only positive figures. In December 2002, they took a simple step that had profound implications: They decided not to offer advance guidance on their quarterly results at all. Although other companies had done this before, Coke was the first major company to do so and it set a precedent for others, like McDonald's, which followed shortly thereafter. "We believe that establishing short-term guidance prevents a more meaningful focus on the strategic initiatives that a company is taking to build its business and succeed over the long run," said Coca-Cola chairman and CEO Douglas Daft. "We are quite comfortable measuring our progress as we achieve it, instead of focusing on the establishment and attainment of public forecasts," he said. "Our share owners are best served by this because we should not run our business based on short-term expectations. We are managing this business for the long term." Another unexpected result of this trend is that analysts will have to conduct their own independent studies of companies rather than relying on numbers given them by the companies themselves.

By considering a range of solutions, not just the traditional ones, Coke's management is steering a course toward what they think is best for the company and its shareholders.

It Pays to Start Education Early

It has been demonstrated that ongoing education is crucial to business success, and starting early is a critical factor. Establishing good learning habits begins in childhood. Local companies that support community school systems benefit because they are able to choose employees from a pool of well-educated residents. Apple Computer understands this concept and puts it into action in its Apples for Education program, in which schools are offered computers at low cost through credit points obtained when student families make purchases at local supermarkets.

WHAT KIND OF CORPORATE STUDENT ARE YOU?

"There are four kinds of students. There is the sponge, the funnel, the strainer and the sieve."[1]

The sponge learner sucks up everything that comes along—the good, the bad, and the in-between. This student makes no distinctions among what he learns. The funnel student learns everything quickly but doesn't retain anything; it simply runs right out. The strainer remembers only the least important of everything he learns as he filters the material.

It's best to be a sieve student. In ancient times, sieves were used to separate the worthless bran from the fine flour. So, too, a sieve student retains the important points and lets the extraneous material flow out.

[1] Avot, 5, 25

Studies show that children who attend preschool do better in kindergarten than those who do not. Researchers say that children not only get a jump start on some basic reading and math skills but also benefit from being introduced to the idea of a formal teaching environment.

Companies that offer preschool payment benefits to employees reap later benefits for themselves.

The Jewish community in Jerusalem began what may have been the world's first compulsory centralized school system. The Talmud is replete with references to the importance of starting education young, when children are ready and willing to learn. Rav said to Rabbi Samuel ben Shilath, "Before the age of six do not accept pupils. From that age you can accept them, however, and stuff them with Torah like an ox."[3] Modern studies also show us that children are capable of learning at an earlier age than was originally thought. Compared to children a generation ago, many of today's kindergarten students are reading and writing before the end of their first year at school.

Educators also know that children can learn many things more easily than adults—especially foreign languages. They are more open to learning than adults because they have not yet established prejudices. In this vein, Elisha ben Abuyah implored everyone to be more like children in their learning habits: "If one learns like a child, what is he like? Like ink written on clean paper. If one learns like an old man, what is that like? Like ink written on blotted paper."[4] "Blotted paper" is a reference to papyrus, which was used over and over because it was expensive. By the time the last person used it, the words were often illegible because the old writing could still be seen. This sage exhorts adults to remain open in their ability to learn new things and not to become set in their ways.

During the period of wholesale computerization of companies in the 1960s and 1970s, many older workers refused to let go of their prejudices about the newfangled computers. Many accepted early retirement rather than learn a new way of doing their jobs. Unlike their grandparents, most children today are comfortable with computers at first introduction. This is a good indication that companies should begin training and education for their newer workers before these employees become too comfortably settled in habits and procedures that make critical and original thinking difficult.

LEARNING HAS NO LIMITS

The Talmudic rabbis debated and argued, and nothing was off-limits as long as the goal was deeper study and learning. The following humorous tale is told about four rabbis, three of whose opinions about a piece of scripture were opposed to that of another. Even if God were to take sides in such a debate, the learning process must continue until it concludes to the satisfaction of everyone involved.

Four rabbis were debating a passage in the Torah. Three of them lined up on one side of the argument, but they could not persuade the fourth to agree with them. The fourth rabbi insisted that the majority was wrong and declared, "I know that God agrees with me. If I'm correct, the Almighty will make a storm cloud to appear in this blue sky as a sign." Just then, a dark thundercloud materialized over the heads of the four rabbis and, just as suddenly, it disappeared. "See," proclaimed the rabbi, "I told you I was right."

The other rabbis still were unconvinced and said that the cloud could be a natural occurrence. The dissenting rabbi was becoming excited and said, "If I am right, I ask God to cause a storm cloud to appear and pour rain."

Again, a storm cloud appeared in the previously cloudless sky, and heavy rain fell. "See," the rabbi said, "I'm right and this proves it."

The other three rabbis stuck to their opinion, saying that both phenomena could be explained by natural events.

Just then, the sky turn black, lightning flashed, and thunder crashed. A booming voice from above said, "He's right!" An instant later, the sky was blue and clear again. The fourth rabbi looked at the other three with a huge grin.

But one rabbi responded, "So what? It's still three against two."

Information versus Knowledge

Although rote learning of the Torah isn't discounted—memorization is used for many of the lessons—children as well as adults are expected to really think about what they're learning. They are encouraged to understand the meaning behind the words that they are committing to memory.

In recent years, we've seen the pendulum swing back toward phonics as a way to teach children reading skills, as opposed to the "whole language" method that was in favor for about a decade. The whole language method teaches children to memorize what entire words look like so they can decipher them again. Many educators considered this a way to produce fast results, and it appeared to bolster the self-esteem of the learners—kids looked like they were reading—but the effects didn't last. Because they were not taught the basics of how letters and letter combinations sounded, students couldn't progress with their reading skills; they lacked the building blocks. Students reached upper grades and some even graduated without really learning how to read. It's simplistic to blame all children's reading problems on whole language instruction, but the method hasn't withstood the test of time. Most school systems are phasing out the whole language approach in favor of phonics.

Companies, too, should follow this example and teach employees how to think rather than insisting on blind adherence to manuals and instructions in order to produce quick results.

Along these lines, companies should encourage employees to understand the difference between information and knowledge. Rabbi Elazar ben Azaryah noted, "Where there is no understanding, there is no knowledge."[5] The difference between information and knowledge is rather a new concept in corporations. It has recently been embraced by forward-thinking companies as the discipline of *competitive intelligence*, and it cuts to the essence of what many people think of as the information age. However, we don't live in the information age anymore; we live in the age of knowledge. There is so much information available— government documents, media, the Internet—that information has become a commodity, like the raw materials used in manufacturing. Without analyzing this information, which transforms it into knowledge, it is almost worthless.

Imagine two stockbrokers. Each has a pager that provides instantaneous share prices, trends, volumes, and so on. They get the same information about a particular company's stocks at the same time, and each makes a trade. One stockbroker makes a million dollars, but the other loses a million dollars. What was the difference? Same raw information, same time—but one of them parlayed the information into usable knowledge and the other did not.

LEARNING MUST HAVE PRACTICAL APPLICATIONS

"The one who studies in order to teach will be enabled to study and teach. The one who studies in order to practice will be enabled to study and to teach, to observe and to practice."[1]

Learning for learning's sake is not enough, says Rabbi Yohannan. The rabbis have little respect for people who spend a lifetime learning but neither transmit their knowledge by teaching nor apply what they've learned to their personal and professional lives. In corporate environments, it is crucial that training be focused on increasing workers' skills and knowledge as they pertain directly to the job. Learning extraneous material may be interesting and can serve as a change of pace or a beneficial mental exercise, but *all* educational experience, ultimately, should be put into practice.

[1]Avot, 4, 5

The Talmud teaches that raw information is worthless unless it is turned into knowledge. Modern educators call this process analysis; the Talmud calls it understanding.

Group Learning

In his seminal book, *The Fifth Discipline* (Doubleday, 1994), Peter Senge emphasized the importance of group learning for an organization to become a true learning organization. Senge wrote: "Individual learning at some level is irrelevant for organizational learning.... Teams must tap the potential for many minds to be more intelligent than one mind...though team learning involves individual skills and areas of understanding, it is a collective discipline."

The Talmud also emphasizes that people should study in groups, because true learning comes as the result of asking questions and receiving answers, which can't be accomplished alone. In addition, so much of what people read (in the Talmud, for sure) needs additional explanation from someone who is more learned.

One of the latest corporate training trends is Internet learning, in which employees learn through Web-based educational materials. Employers like this method because it is inexpensive, and employees like it because it can be done most any time. The downside is that there may not be anyone available to answer students' questions when they arise. Another shortcoming is that students do not have the opportunity to learn from the questions of other students taking the same course—there is no cross-pollination of ideas.

As the Talmud sages would probably suggest, successful Web-based learning systems should include an online instructor as well as a mechanism—an Internet forum, perhaps—to enable students to learn from other students.

SMALL CLASS SIZES ARE BEST

"The number of pupils to be assigned to each teacher is twenty-five. If there are fifty, we appoint two teachers. If there are forty, we appoint an assistant, at the expense of the town."[1]

The ancient rabbis believed in group learning, but they also understood the importance of small class size. Although these numbers apply mainly to the teaching of children, they can also be applied to adult learning situations. The smaller the class size, the better. Learning that takes place in a large auditorium or lecture hall filled with students can be effective, but the most efficient learning environment is a small group.

[1]Bava Batra, 21b

Characteristics of Teachers

In Jewish tradition, the most revered job in the world is that of teacher. The word *rabbi* means "teacher," and it's no surprise that the Talmudic rabbis wrote extensively about what makes a great teacher. These ancient lessons are useful today in choosing educators for corporate training programs as well as community schools and universities. Some of these characteristics may seem obvious, but it's worth pointing them out, as any employee who has endured a poor instructor knows.

One of the most important characteristics of good teachers is that they practice what they preach. The rabbis had no respect for scholars who taught the Torah but didn't practice its tenets. A good teacher's commitment extended beyond teaching to his daily life. Likewise, the rabbis had little interest in teachers who didn't live in the real world. Recall that the ancient rabbis also held other jobs—usually in manual labor—which helped them keep in touch with what was going on in the world of daily commerce.

ENCOURAGEMENT

"When you punish a pupil, only hit him with a shoe lace."[1]

The ancient rabbis were very clear about what made a good teacher great. Not only should teachers possess wisdom, but they should be slow to anger and exercise a high level of patience with their pupils. The Talmud stresses that learning should be enjoyable, not a chore, despite the hard work it requires. The best teachers understand this and never punish poor students for making mistakes in their studies.

It's likewise important that corporate instructors allow their students to make mistakes, even though this is generally not characteristic of corporations. Students who don't learn as quickly or as thoroughly as others should not be penalized.

[1]Bava Batra, 21b

In today's business environment, the most effective teachers are those people who have actually worked in the industry about which they are teaching. No amount of book learning can replace real-life experiences. Moreover, more experienced workers have an obligation as well to pass on knowledge to newer or younger workers. Not only does this constitute a good deed, but it serves as the source of a feeling of accomplishment for teacher and learner alike.

In today's business environment, the most effective teachers are those people who have actually worked in the industry about which they are teaching. No amount of book learning can replace real-life experiences.

The rabbis were critical of people who were knowledgeable but did not use that gift of knowledge to solve real-world problems or help others through teaching. As Rabbi Elazar explained, "What is a person like, whose wisdom exceeds his deeds? He is like a tree with many branches but few roots and the wind comes and picks it up and overturns it. He shall be like a lonely juniper tree in the desert. He will not see any good come his way but shall live in parched places in the wilderness."[6]

Just like money, knowledge is wasted by being stuck in one place. Ideally, knowledge and wisdom should be moving among people who can then use them to build prosperity and perform good deeds.

Summary—Lesson Nine

1. Learning is a lifelong process. People must continue their education throughout their careers.

2. Companies benefit by establishing educational programs for employees. Companies also reap dividends by helping to educate children in their communities.

3. Employee learning should be focused on critical thinking and not education by rote.

4. Students should differentiate between information and knowledge. Information is a commodity and assumes value only after it is filtered and analyzed and becomes knowledge.

5. Group learning is more effective than learning alone, because education involves asking questions and exchanging ideas.

6. The most effective corporate trainers are those who have practical, on-the-job industry experience.

NUMBERED REFERENCES

[1]Avot, 1, 13
[2]Avot, 5, 25
[3]Bava Batra, 21a
[4]Avot, 4, 25
[5]Avot, 3, 21
[6]Avot, 3, 22

Charity Means More
Than Just Giving

Charity is equal to all the commandments in the world combined.

—RAV ASSI[1]

To the Talmudic rabbis, charity is not solely an act of kindness or compassion; it is also an act of justice. They saw charity as a *legal* obligation that *must* be performed by all individuals and businesses.

Further insight can be gleaned from the derivations of the words used for this act. The English word *charity* is derived from the Latin word *caritas*, which means "love." In Greek, the word for love is *philo*, the root of *philanthropy*. Both of these derivations convey the idea that charity is an act of love toward other people.

On the other hand, the Hebrew word for charity is *tzedakah*, from the word *tzedek*, which means "just," as in the word *justice*. In Judaism, giving charity is not an act of love, but an act of justice, a way of adjusting the playing field that moves the universe toward fairness.

By many Talmudic accounts, charity is the strongest force in the universe. The sages considered it more powerful and more important than all the sacrifices ever brought to the ancient Temples. It is said that giving charity can even save us from death, as this parable of the sheep illustrates.

Two sheep were trying to cross a river to reach fresh grass. One sheep had recently been shorn and had no trouble swimming. The other one was loaded with wool and sank under its weight when its coat absorbed the water. The rabbis remarked that this story shows the importance of giving your money away before your death so it may benefit others. If not, it may "sink" with you.[2]

GIVE WHILE YOU CAN

A blind beggar stopped two men walking on the road. One of the men gave the beggar some money, but the other did not.

Soon, the Angel of Death approached both travelers, and said, "He who gave to the beggar need not fear me for another fifty years, but the other will die soon."

"May I return and give money to the beggar now?" said the traveler who hadn't given charity to the beggar.

"No," said the Angel of Death. "A boat is examined for holes and cracks before it sets sail, not after it has departed."[1]

[1]Midrash, from Meil Tzedakah

Why Are There Needy People?

The question arose among the sages: Why did God make poor people in the first place? Why are we tasked with being God's stewards, with the obligation and responsibility of redistributing wealth to those who need it? Why doesn't God do it?

The rabbis pondered this and agreed that charity affords us a unique opportunity to make the world a better place—"to repair it," as the rabbis noted—to complete God's job of creation. This is not to say that God purposely made some people poor only so that others could give charity; nevertheless, there will always be poor people in the world. Charitable giving enables us to extend ourselves to those who are less fortunate as a result of their bad luck or bad choices.

All of us possess free will and face daily decisions about what to do with our money. Giving charity is an indication that we've made a righteous choice about how to spend our (God's) money, and we are blessed for doing so. The rabbis liked to say, "Although the wine belongs to the owner, thanks are given to the butler."[3] In other words, the world's wealth belongs to the Almighty, but people dole it out. This concept of people's stewardship appears throughout the Talmud, and applies not only to money but to environmental issues as you've seen. It bears repeating that all wealth comes from God, and it is up to all of us to use wisdom and justice in spending it.

Charity Etiquette

Because charity plays such an important part in "repairing" the world, Talmudic tradition has elevated it to an art form with intricate rules and procedures. For example, charity should be tendered regardless of who needs it. Donors are not to discriminate against a person who doesn't work because he is lazy as opposed to someone who is unable to work as the result of an injury. It's not our place to determine why someone needs charity—only that the person needs our help. We also should extend charity to those needy people whom we might regard as offensive or impudent. Again, this should not factor into our decision to give charity.

Although the Talmud says it's acceptable to investigate people who are asking for charity, to ascertain whether they are truly needy, there should be no investigation or hesitation if they are in dire need. The

BAD CHARITY

"Is giving charity sometimes bad? Yes, when one gives charity to a man in the street or to a woman in secret."[1]

This most interesting observation discusses the Talmudic rabbis' vigilance about not causing harm to the recipient. Giving charity to a person in public can be humiliating to the recipient and should be avoided. However, when a man gives money to a woman in secret, especially in her home, outsiders may get the impression that something improper is going on.

[1]Hagigah, 5a

rabbis said that when a starving person asks for food, he is to be given it immediately. If a person asks for clothes, you may, if you wish, investigate him to make sure he is deserving, but whether the person turns out to be truly needy or a fraud, the good deed of charity enjoys the same worth. This is an intriguing point of view on the rabbis' part. Even if we find out after the fact that a charitable organization wasted or misused donor money, as happened several years ago with some Goodwill Industries officials, our act of giving is still valid and honorable.

The Talmud also specifies the order in which people are to receive charity. First on the list are those in our own family or company. Next come those in our community, and then those who live farther away.

One company that believes charity begins at home is Hallmark Cards. Rather than sending charitable donations to distant locations, Hallmark funnels its contributions and volunteer resources to organizations based in and providing services to the metropolitan Kansas City area and other communities where Hallmark facilities are located. In early 1979, Chairman Donald Hall and the Kansas City Civic Council commissioned a study, which resulted in the creation of the Kansas City Neighborhood Alliance, now a major leader in the rejuvenation of housing in the urban core.

The rabbis made sure that donors understood that an overriding factor in giving charity is preserving the recipient's dignity. It is demeaning enough to accept charity, and a needy person should not be subjected to further indignities. In ancient Jerusalem, people who had extra food to share would place a cloth outside their doors at dinnertime. This signaled that the meal was under way and that the owners were willing to accept guests. Poor people could enter the house and feel invited, thus preserving their dignity.

IT'S THE THOUGHT THAT COUNTS

"A man may give liberally, but if he gives begrudgingly and wounds the heart of the poor, his gift is in vain. It has lost the characteristic of charity. Another man may give little, but if he gives with his heart, he and his act are blessed."[1]

Although *any* act of charity is a righteous event, to give without regret and without humiliating the recipient is considered more virtuous.

[1]Bava Batra, 9a

The Top Eight Ways to Give Charity

Maimonides ranked eight different ways to give charity—from the best to the worst—with the goal of maintaining the recipient's dignity at the top of the list. Notice that this speaks to a company's obligation to help individuals through employment and assist other companies through partnerships and loans.

1. **Providing assistance by helping people find work, offering a loan, or entering into a partnership in order to help start or maintain a business.** Helping people and organizations increase

community prosperity is the best kind of charity because there is an opportunity for lasting growth.

2. **Providing assistance in such a way that neither the recipient nor the receiver knows the other.** Giving anonymously through a third party ensures that the recipient is not humiliated or embarrassed.

3. **Giving such that the donor knows who receives the charity, but the recipient doesn't know the donor.** This is the case when a needy person receives a gift from an organization that locates needy recipients. For example, a donor might learn about a needy child through a written profile, but the child is not told anything about the donor.

4. **Giving such that the recipient knows the donor, but the donor doesn't know who receives his gift.** This scenario is possible if a third-party charitable organization is used, but it's rare in contemporary times.

5. **Giving such that each party is aware of the other, but the gift is unsolicited.** Giving money to a street person is a good example of this type of charity.

6. **Giving such that each party is aware of the other, and the gift is given in response to a request.** If the street person asks for money, this scenario applies.

7. **Giving such that each party is aware of the other and the gift is offered in response to a request, but it is less than should be given.** For example, a beggar asks for a dollar, and the donor gives 50 cents.

8. **Giving grudgingly.** This kind of giving often occurs in response to aggressive panhandling; the donor feels coerced into giving and does so only to ward off further begging.

Remember that we are not obligated to give more charity than we can afford, no matter what the situation. Maimonides warns that people should not give too much to charity so that they become impoverished and are forced to rely on charity themselves.

GIVING IT ALL AWAY

"Charity is an obligation, but there are limits. To give away all of your possessions and make yourself poor is prohibited."[1]

"Even a poor person who lives off charity is expected to give charity."[2]

[1]Ketubot, 50a
[2]Gittin, 7a

One approach that follows Maimonides's first rule is the Shefa Fund's Tzedec Campaign, part of a movement in the American Jewish community to fight poverty through community banking and investing. Philadelphia-based Tzedec encourages American Jews and their organizations—including synagogues, foundations, and federations—to make deposits and invest in community-based financial institutions that serve low-income people. These deposits and investments support affordable housing, small business development, child care programs, and other social services in neighborhoods where they are most needed. Since its inception in 1997, Tzedec has catalyzed more than $12 million to help people in low-income neighborhoods help themselves.

Special Obligations of Businesses

Businesses have a unique obligation to help the poor because of their often superior financial position in the community. In Biblical times, when landowners harvested their fields, they were obligated to leave the corners alone. They were also not permitted to go back and pick up fruit or vegetables dropped along the way during harvesting. The leavings were for the poor.

Many restaurants and caterers have tried to follow this example by offering leftover food to homeless shelters. However, because of our litigious society, some were afraid to do this until municipalities passed laws that protected them from liability if someone were to become ill from the donated food. One organization that does this is Philadelphia's

GIVE THE GIFT OF TIME

"He who gives a small coin to a poor person receives six blessings. He who speaks kindly to him, gives him words to cheer him up, receives eleven blessings."[1]

It is often much easier for us to give money to people rather than our time. This passage reminds us that the gift of our time may be more precious than that of our money.

One company that understands the importance of giving money *and* time to charities is the Timberland Company in Stratham, New Hampshire, which produces outdoor apparel. Its Path of Service program gives all of the company's full-time U.S. employees 40 hours of paid leave to perform community service. The program began in 1992 and offered employees 16 hours for charitable work, but as the levels of interest and participation grew, the program expanded to 40 hours. Today, the Path of Service program is the cornerstone of the company's community involvement and contributes more than 100,000 total hours of service annually by employees. According to company officials, the commitment so far has benefited over 200 community organizations in 13 countries, 26 states, and 73 cities. Nearly 95 percent of Timberland's U.S. employees use at least some of their Path of Service benefit.

[1]Bava Batra, 9b

Philabundance, which picks up perishable leftover foods from restaurants and caterers and delivers it to 200 charitable organizations, including shelters, emergency kitchens, community food cupboards, and social service agencies. Since 1984, the group has provided food for over 60 million meals.

Other programs are springing up around the United States with the aim of helping companies donate leftovers from production processes. Groups such as the National Association for the Exchange of Industrial Resources accepts donations of new, excess inventory and distributes this to 5,500 schools and nonprofit organizations around the United States. Since 1977, the group has given away more than $1.7 billion worth of merchandise. Corporate donors include Microsoft, Gillette, Fuller Industries, Sauder Furniture, Esselte Pendaflex, General Electric, and thousands of other manufacturers, wholesalers, and distributors.

Charity is a moral and ethical obligation, and no other reason for giving should be necessary. However, companies often try to quantify their charity in order to increase employee morale, qualify for tax write-offs, lower their refuse costs, and enhance awareness in the community that the company is a good neighbor.

According to the Talmudic rabbis, whether a person or company gives charity for self-serving reasons or for more righteous reasons, the recipient is still blessed by the act and the recipient still reaps the benefit.

Ulterior motives should not concern us. According to the Talmudic rabbis, whether a person or company gives charity for self-serving reasons or for more righteous reasons, the recipient is still blessed by the act and the recipient still reaps the benefit.

DOES CHARITY REACH YOUR BOTTOM LINE?

Two-thirds of consumers say that if price and quality are equal, they are likely to switch to a brand or retailer that gives to a good cause, according to a 1999 study done for Cone Inc.

Employees like it, too. The Boston-based marketing firm found that nearly 90 percent of employees of companies that promote worthy causes and charities feel a strong sense of loyalty to the firm, compared to 67 percent at companies that don't.

Cisco Systems, in San Jose, California, was forced to lay off about 6,000 full-time workers in April 2001. The company came up with a unique plan to help local charities and the furloughed workers in the process. The company paid the workers one-third of their normal salaries if they agreed to work for a local nonprofit organization for a year. They also received benefits and stock options and will be the first to be rehired when the economy recovers. This plan will pay off directly for Cisco since many of these workers will still be in Cisco's local available labor pool when business improves.

Although charity in general is an obligation, there's a different kind of charity that is not obligatory and so, in some ways, is greater than charity, the rabbis said. The Hebrew phrase for this type of giving is *Gemilut Chessed,* which means "acts of loving-kindness." The best way to explain the difference between *Gemilut Chessed* and charity, aside from the Talmudic legal imperative of charity, is that acts of loving-kindness are not performed with money but with a person's time. Giving money to a sick person is charity. Spending time with that person is an act of loving-kindness. The sages also noted that charity is given only to the poor, but acts of loving-kindness are given to both rich and poor. Another distinction is that charity can be given only to the living, but acts of loving-kindness can be done for the dead as well as for the living—for example, preparing a proper burial or bestowing a posthumous award. Another distinction between charity and acts of loving-kindness is that acts of charity could lead to repayment of the good deed. Acts of loving-kindness are done without any hope or expectation of repayment.

In other words, my bread is an issue of material concern to me. My neighbor's bread is an issue of my spiritual concern.

Rabbi Israel Salanter, founder of the nineteenth-century Lithuanian Mussar movement, which stressed ethics and self-improvement, summarized the subject of charity: "A person should be more concerned with spiritual than with material matters, but another person's material welfare is his own spiritual concern." In other words, my bread is an issue of material concern to me. My neighbor's bread is an issue of my spiritual concern.

Summary—Lesson Ten

1. Charity is everyone's obligation. Donations kept close to home are the most blessed.

2. Helping an individual or company with a loan, a job, or a partnership is the most noble form of charity.

3. Charity should not be given based on the recipient's race, creed, religion, or attitude.

NUMBERED REFERENCES

[1]Bava Batra, 9a
[2]Gittin, 61a
[3]Bava Kama, 92a

The Ultimate Business Secret of the Rabbis: Reputation

"There are three crowns: the crown of learning, the crown of the priesthood and the crown of royalty, but the crown of a good name exceeds them all."

—RABBI SIMEON[1]

An atheist came to the great sage Hillel, willing to be converted to Judaism on the condition that he be taught the entire contents of the Torah while standing on one foot. Hillel accepted the challenge. "What is hateful to you, do not do to your fellow man. This is the whole of Torah," said Hillel. "Everything else is commentary."

In similar fashion, the Talmudic rabbis would sum up the secret of business success in one word:

REPUTATION

A good reputation—or "good name," as the rabbis called it—is what people and companies acquire when they follow a strict ethical code. This code includes the ways in which they view the roles of work and money, buy and sell, protect the environment, engage in fair and honest competition, and deliver high-quality, innovative products and services. Having a good name in business also means being compassionate, tough, decisive, fair-minded, and clever—all within ethical parameters. In short, a good reputation is gained by following the business lessons you just read.

Clients, customers, government regulators, and the courts gain confidence in a company and its workers through its reputation as an honest and upright practitioner. This, in turn, attracts more customers, more profits, and greater prosperity. Cultivating a good name takes courage, a belief in oneself, a belief in the company's products and services, a spiritual foundation, and the strength to follow a path that may not always be parallel to that of others.

Reputations are built slowly and steadily—product by product, transaction by transaction, and sale by sale. Although a good name can be gained, it can also be lost through unethical business activities, dishonesty, and poor products and service. A reputation can likewise be lost as the result of malicious gossip and rumors, as you'll see later.

Pundits may discuss "reputational management" and offer ideas on how companies can go about strengthening their reputations through public relations campaigns or advertising efforts, but these are hollow efforts in the long run. Reputation can only be built cumulatively, through protracted hard work, real deeds, and exemplary actions—not as the result of window dressing or short-term, high-impact efforts.

Reputation can only be built cumulatively, through protracted hard work, real deeds, and exemplary actions—not as the result of window dressing or short-term, high-impact efforts.

How a Strong Reputation Saved Intel

We all make mistakes and suffer lapses in judgment. A strong reputation can be a savior during such times of crisis.

EXXON AND MOBIL: GUILT BY ASSOCIATION

Once a reputation is lost, it is nearly impossible to reclaim. Even 10 years after the environmental tragedy of the Exxon *Valdez* oil spill, the company's reputation—tarnished by its handling of the incident—still haunts it. Company officials have considered an ad campaign to highlight its environmental programs but decided against it because they didn't think people would believe it.

Many consumers continue to boycott Exxon gas stations, and the taint has spread to Mobil, which the company bought in 1999. "I would get a tow truck before I would use Exxon or Mobil gas," Claudia Lieber, a Long Island paralegal told the *Wall Street Journal* in 2001. She added, "I used Mobil all the time before the merger but I believe I must take a stand over that horrific, disgraceful Alaskan oil spill by not giving Exxon or Mobil another cent."

According to a study by Harris Interactive and the Reputation Institute, Lieber is not alone. Nearly half of those familiar with Exxon continue to give it a low grade when it comes to corporate reputation.

After years spent building a reputation for quality products and name recognition (the "Intel Inside" trademark had become a symbol of quality in computers), Intel customers discovered in 1994 that its premier product, the Pentium chip, contained a flaw. The fault was minuscule and affected only those who engaged in high-precision, rocket-science-type calculations. Initially, Intel denied that the problem existed; however, consumers grew angry as they read and heard evidence to the contrary. Intel decided, begrudgingly, that only customers who had a need for such precision calculations—such as scientists and researchers—should be offered a free replacement. Consumer ire grew.

Eventually, IBM, one of Intel's major clients, stopped selling computers with Pentium processors. End users—consumers and businesses—stopped buying computers that contained Pentium chips, motivated partly by anger that the company didn't think they needed to supply the update universally and partly by their confusion about the severity of the problem with the chip.

Intel's stock dropped nearly 15 percent during the crisis, and the company lost more money as a result of postponed sales than if it had simply offered free chips to anyone who had asked for them when the crisis was first discovered.

Company president Andrew Grove publicly apologized, saying, "We decided what was good and what was not good for our customer when we had to replace the Pentium. It turns out that consumers highly resent it when a company presumes to judge the quality of its products on their behalf."

During this incident, the *Washington Post* noted: "Intel has lost some of its reputation with the revelation that its Pentium chip is flawed. Not only has Intel's reputation for quality been compromised, but analysts say its handling of the situation has been very poor."

Intel was fortunate that its long-term reputation was strong enough for the company to survive, once it admitted its mistake. A company with a lesser reputation would have suffered irreparable damage.

The Dollars and Cents of Reputation

Charles Fombrun, executive director of the Reputation Institute and research professor of management at New York University's Stern School of Business and author of *Reputation: Realizing Value from the Corporate Image* (Harvard Business School Press, 1996), defines reputation—or *reputational capital,* as he prefers to call it—as "intangible wealth that is closely related to what accountants call 'goodwill' and marketers term 'brand equity.'" Companies with strong reputations enjoy a competitive advantage over rivals, because it allows them to charge premium prices for products and services and enjoy lower marketing costs. It also allows them to attract highly motivated, productive workers; quality suppliers; and loyal customers.

AT&T is a good example of this phenomenon. During the later 1970s and early 1980s, before it was split into the local Bell companies and the long-distance arm, AT&T was faced with competition from

REPUTATION SAVES A SMALL COMPANY

A good reputation saved Randi Korn & Associates, a small museum consulting company. About 10 years ago, a competitor emerged, and Korn saw a dip in her business. This new entrant had just published a book popular in the museum world, had a larger staff, and was flashier. "My friends told me I should just keep doing what I was doing. From their perspective my company had integrity and a reputation for focusing on clients' needs and producing quality work that helps practitioners make decisions. They believed that we would not just survive, but we would be a strong force and rise to the top of the profession, because ultimately quality matters," said Korn.

Her instincts told her to continue to feed the passions of her staff, be painfully honest but sensitive when the data are negative, acknowledge errors, be patient when working with novice clients, and care about every client and project no matter how big or small. At times, she found it difficult to do this because she feared making a wrong move. However, her friends—and her instincts—were right. She says, "Every year, for the last five years, the number of referrals we receive rises exponentially. People call because others tell them to or they read one of our reports; sometimes people call because they were dissatisfied with our competitor. Whatever the reason, and even with repeat clients, we approach each new project with the goal of producing a quality product that responds to a client's needs."

discount long-distance providers like Sprint and MCI. Although the long-distance telephone lines were similar—and in some cases, exactly the same—millions of customers stuck with the higher-priced AT&T service because of the company's excellent reputation. Its market share didn't begin to erode until court proceedings revealed that AT&T had acted illegally in keeping out long-distance competitors. Even then, many consumers remembered the "Ma Bell" that had served them so well in the past, and they continued as customers longer than competitors had predicted.

Reputation has also been vital to the success of legendary investor Warren Buffett, CEO of conglomerate Berkshire Hathaway, who once told his managers, "If you lose dollars for the firm by bad decisions, I will be very understanding. If you lose reputation for the firm, I will be ruthless." In his annual letter to CEOs of the companies owned by Berkshire Hathaway, Buffett once wrote: "We can afford to lose money. We can afford to lose a lot of money, but we can't afford to lose our reputation." Buffett has built his reputation over many decades and remains vigilant about protecting it.

Even Alan Greenspan, the Federal Reserve Board chairman who orchestrated the single best economic period in the history of the United States, told Harvard students at their 1999 commencement, "I cannot speak for others whose psyches I may not be able to comprehend, but in my working life I have found no greater satisfaction than achieving success through honest dealings and strict adherence to the view that for you to gain, those you deal with should gain as well. Human relations—be they personal or professional—should not be zero sum games. And beyond the personal sense of satisfaction, having a reputation for fair dealing is a profoundly practical virtue. We call it 'good will' in business and add it to our balance sheets." Greenspan understands not only the dollars-and-sense aspect of reputation but the psychological importance as well.

Reputation is acquiring even more importance as competition becomes keener and consumers grow better informed. One result of the total quality movement of the 1980s is that products in general are better than ever, but there's a downside for sellers and manufacturers. Consumers have a difficult time discriminating among products as the quality bar continually rises. As the differentiation among products narrows, consumers are relying more heavily on name recognition and reputation to guide their purchases.

For example, in 1995 Duke Power, in Charlotte, North Carolina, asked customers to rate them on 18 corporate attributes that included ethics, environmental consciousness, and customer responsiveness. But why would a regulated company care about reputation? Vice President Roberta Bowman said in *Industry Week* (February 3, 1997), "As electricity becomes commoditized, the only thing that will distinguish one company from another will be its name and reputation that it conjures up." Most likely, electrical power won't always be a monopoly business, and Duke is preparing for the day when it must compete on the basis of reputation because the products will all be equal.

Dollar amounts can be placed on reputation. The technical term for this, which is accepted in accounting circles, is *goodwill*, and it is quantified when a company is sold. Goodwill is the premium paid for a company over the actual book value of its assets, reflecting the buyer's belief that the company's reputation has some value. Reputation is a combination of the company's name recognition, history, trademarks, employees' skills, and all other intangibles. Goodwill is also factored into a company's share price by the market, giving companies with good reputations higher multiples than their peers.

Branding and Cobranding

Harley-Davidson has a line of clothing. Dannon yogurt sells bottled water. Goosebumps, the children's book series, has spawned a line of kid's clothes, backpacks, and snack foods.

A QUANTITATIVE LOOK AT REPUTATION

Research studies linking strong reputations and profitability have increased in frequency since the late 1990s. According to Ernst & Young, the investment community reckons that 30 to 50 percent of a company's value is intangible—mostly driven by reputation-related factors.

At a 1997 conference on corporate reputation hosted by the Stern School of Business, the papers presented showed the effect of reputation on a company's bottom line. A study of 10 company portfolios revealed that investors were willing to pay more for companies with better reputations but with the same levels of risk and return. This lowers a company's cost of capital. A study of 200 business undergraduate students found that they were more attracted to jobs in high-reputation companies. This allows high-reputation companies to hire the best-in-class over their competitors.

The 1998 *Fortune* survey of the most admired companies indicated that the price/earnings ratios of companies with high corporate equity—that is, a great reputation—were 12 percent higher than those with low equity. This translates to a $5 billion increase in market capitalization for the average Fortune 500 company due to the higher reputation.

All these companies are using their reputations and name recognition to sell products from outside of their industry. What does Harley-Davidson know about clothing? What does Goosebumps series author R.L. Stine know about snack foods? Nothing—but consumers associate their names with value and quality, allowing them to begin product line extension simply on the basis of their reputation.

Many companies have chosen to build relationships with other companies that enjoy strong reputations in order to boost their own.

REPUTATION, IMAGE, AND BRANDING:
WHAT'S THE DIFFERENCE?

Reputation, image, and branding are often mistakenly used interchangeably, but they mean different things.

Reputation describes the net image of a company held by stakeholders as well as less-interested parties. It encompasses all of their rational and visceral feelings about the company.

Brand is a label that a company employs on products or services to distinguish itself among its *own* customers.

Image is the cumulative value that a company, store, brand, or product has for a particular customer or demographic group. There are as many images as there are people who experience them because each person sees and feels the image in a different manner.

Although a company can have only one overall reputation, which is consistent for all customers, shareholders, the general public, and the media, it can have many different images and brands.

A company's reputation can help it fortify and extend its brands and images.

Mail Boxes Etc. (MBE), a franchise that packs and mails goods for consumers and businesses, ran advertisements featuring Konica copiers, U.S. Air, Oscar Mayer, and Dutch Boy Paints because of these firms' reputations for quality service and products. The message to consumers is that if these reputable companies are doing business with MBE, it must be better than the competition. In what may be the largest rebranding effort in retail and franchise history in the United States, Mail Boxes Etc. began changing its signs to read "The UPS Store," in April 2003, following the company's purchase by the package delivery company in 2001. UPS bought the 3,300-store franchise, (about 3,000 franchisees have chosen to rebrand) because of its strong neighborhood presence and reputation. UPS will use the stores to help introduce the public to its modernized company logo featuring a stylized shield in place of the older logo showing a bow-tied parcel. Each company will benefit from the other's solid reputation. Likewise, Red Lobster advertises that it uses FedEx to deliver live lobsters to its restaurants. If diners had any doubt about the lobsters' freshness, FedEx's reputation for reliability and on-time delivery would take care of that.

Reputation and the Internet

The rules of success in e-commerce are no different from those in the world of bricks and mortar. You could argue, however, that reputation is even *more important* to Internet businesses because customers can't touch or see the merchandise up close.

The Web's second most visited jewelry site and the most profitable, www.ice.com is owned by the Gniwisch family, who have enjoyed an excellent reputation in the diamond business in the United States and Canada. Both parents, European Jews, survived the Holocaust. They later settled in Montreal, raised six children, and started Delmar Jewelry, one of Canada's largest jewelry manufacturers.

Sons Shmuel and Mayer launched First Canadian Diamond Cutting Works, Canada's first diamond factory. Later, Mayer began a multimillion-dollar diamond business in New York, and Shmuel became a success in real estate and recycling ventures. Apart from their business acumen, Shmuel, Mayer, and siblings Pinny and Moshie draw deeply on their Jewish heritage and are ordained rabbis. Like the ancient rabbis, they work in the real world of business as well.

They learned about the Internet the hard way when they packed up their families—18 people including kids—and relocated to Pasadena, California, to work with the famous Internet incubator Idealab!, which promised $5 million in capital and services for what was then called buyjewels.com. By 2000, the e-commerce bubble had burst, and the families moved back to Montreal after buying back their company, which had changed its name to ice.com.

"The Talmud saved us on many levels because it teaches diversification. We didn't put everything into the internet but kept our other investments and businesses. The Talmud and Bible also remind us that the business world—and especially the internet—is really all about transparency and reputation," Shmuel Gniwisch said. "Everything has to be as true as possible."

Transparency pays off for the Gniwischs. They enjoy a merchandise return rate below 10 percent, compared to 18 to 20 percent for the retail jewelry business. "We give as much information as we can on the buy side, so we don't have to do it on the return side."

Gniwisch said that in the diamond business, your name supersedes you, and it's what you trade on. The worldwide network of dealers known as the Diamond Dealer Club has a blacklist of dishonest people, which is transmitted around the world. "You can lose your reputation in a second," he says. "Money comes and goes, but your name is what you always have."

Losing Reputation through Words

Although a company can lose a good reputation thorough its own misdeeds, it can also lose it as the result of the misdeeds of others. The Talmudic sages were always watchful of the dangers of losing a business reputation because of slander and gossip. In the same way that the Diamond Dealer Club relies on word of mouth to keep members honest, words can also quickly sink a reputation, as the rabbis discussed in great detail.

The rabbis taught: "A person's tongue is more powerful than his sword. A sword can only kill someone who is nearby; a tongue can cause the death of someone who is far away."[2] The sages were referring to defaming someone's reputation, which they likened to a weapon with long-range power. Their use of the word *death* is interesting because it suggests that reputation is so important that to lose it is tantamount to dying.

Gossip and rumormongering were so abhorrent to the rabbis that they established complex rules for what could be said about a person or company to another party. For example, they did not allow discussion of someone's negative character traits, even with a person who had firsthand knowledge of them. They forbade people to make derogatory remarks about someone, even when the information was widely known and caused no harm. Furthermore, they disallowed negative suggestions to be made about a person by means of hand motions, winks, nods, or other gestures. The rabbis even prohibited listening to disparaging remarks about someone. Negative remarks can damage a person's or a company's reputation, but the rabbis also understood that they can cause emotional pain and loss of self-esteem, which is a further reason for prohibiting gossip and rumors. The rabbis recognized that once rumors got started, they were impossible to retract, as the following story demonstrates.

A man spread a rumor about a person with whom he did business and wanted to take it all back after he saw how it had affected the subject of the rumor. He asked the rabbi how to go about retracting his comments.

"Go to the field," the rabbi said, "and spread to the winds the seeds that are in this sack. Then come back to me in a week."

The rumormonger did as he was told and spoke to the rabbi a week later.

"Now, go back to the field and pick up all the seeds and place them back into the bag."

"That's impossible," the man exclaimed. "There were thousands of seeds and many of them have already taken root in the soil."

"Now you understand," the rabbi said. "When we speak badly

about another person, its effect goes far and wide. The damage it causes can never be fully undone."

A contemporary example is the experience of home-product giant Procter & Gamble. Since the early 1980s, the company has spent countless hours and enormous financial resources debunking the rumor that it gives money to satanic organizations. The rumor apparently was started by people who thought the company's logo, which contains a moon and stars, is symbolic of devil worship. Procter & Gamble contends that the rumor was started "for competitive reasons"—in other words, that it was the work of a competing company.

Absolutely none of these accusations about devil worship are true, but the rumor resurfaces every several years and reaches a fever pitch, and the company spends time quelling it. The situation is so acute that the company has devoted many pages on its web site to the matter.

The rumors also say that the president of P&G appeared on the TV programs of Sally Jessy Raphael and Phil Donahue to announce the company's commitment to satanic causes. The truth is that no P&G official has ever appeared on these or any other TV show. The sad fact is that the rumors have made it impossible for any P&G official to go on a talk show because it would only make matters worse. The frequently asked questions (FAQs) section of P&G's web site posts the following exchange:

Q: Why doesn't your President go on a talk show to denounce the rumor?

A: We wish it were that simple. The problem is then we couldn't say our President never appeared on a TV program. Just think about it, if well-meaning individuals are spreading rumors when we haven't even been on talk shows, imagine what might be said if any of our executives actually appeared on them. Words might be taken out of context and only fuel the rumors.

Unfortunately, P&G is in an untenable situation, like the man in the story who scattered the seeds to the winds.

The Talmudic rabbis maintain that it's up to each of us to build and protect our own reputation and that of our company. In the final analysis, a good name is the prime factor in business success and the only element that endures long after the people who created it are gone.

In the final analysis, a good name is the prime factor in business success and the only element that endures long after the people who created it are gone.

Echoing Rabbi Simeon, Rabbi Tanhuma reminds us of this: "You will find that a person is given three names—one that his parents call him, one that his fellow human beings call him and one that he acquires for himself. The one that he acquires for himself is better than all the others."[3]

NUMBERED REFERENCES

[1]Avot, 4, 13
[2]Sabbath, 15b
[3]Midrash Tanhuma

A NOTE ON TRANSLATION
AND COMMENTATORS

The main source of quotations and stories for this book is the Babylonian Talmud, and they come mostly from the *Soncino* version, which was first printed in the late 1400s in Italy. I made extensive use of the CD-ROM version published by Jewish Life & Dakva Corporation and Judaica Press. In some cases I used their English translation, and in others I used my own. I also employed the Steinsaltz Edition of the Talmud, published by Random House, for its text, commentary, and translations. Other editions and translations of the Talmud were also employed.

Because the Babylonian Talmud was written in East Aramaic language but also contains passages in Hebrew, and the Palestinian Talmud was written in West Aramaic language but also has many words from Greek, translations into modern English will differ. I endeavored to maintain the original flavor and tone of the rabbis' statements while keeping them acceptable to modern ears.

There are many statements in the Talmud and Mishnah that are unattributed. The rule among scholars is that unattributed comments in the Mishnah that originated from consensus opinion were from Rabbi Judah Ha-Nasi (Judah the Prince), who played the largest role in compiling the Mishnah. Mishnah containing disagreements but without an attributed rabbi came from Rabbi Meir. Unattributed comments in the Talmud are from Ravina or Rav Ashi. I have kept these conventions. Often, the same statements are repeated by several different people in various sections. I have tried to use the first reference.

I also have included commentary from post-Talmudic scholars such as Rashi and Maimonides.

A SHORT HISTORY OF THE TALMUD

Writing It Down

Around 70 C.E., Jewish culture and learning flourished in Palestine, and a group of scholars known as *Tannaim* ("ones who study") became prominent. Not anonymous like many earlier Jewish scholars, they had followings and were regarded as celebrities. Among them was the famous Hillel and the not quite as familiar Shammai. Each of these scholars had his own school of thought with differing views. They debated, argued, and split hairs, and their lively discussions brought to life a new era of learning led by a group of scholars and rabbis whose names appear in the Talmud.

Each contributor to these discussions had a unique voice and gave his own opinion on the subjects under consideration. One of the most important was Rabbi Judah Ha-Nasi. Rabbi Judah "the Prince," as he was known, presided over the Sanhedrin, Judaism's highest judicial and legislative body. A wealthy man, he took a less antagonistic tack with the Roman authorities than some of his contemporaries, and this led to an era of tolerance and sometimes even benevolence toward Jews. Rabbi Judah knew that this feeling of goodwill wouldn't last forever, so he launched a long-term project during this peaceful period. Judah sought to organize the Mishnah, making them easier to teach and learn.

It is not clear whether the Mishnah were written down at this point or if they continued to be presented orally—or both. The Tannaim continued to memorize the Mishnah, transforming each man into a "living book."

After Rabbi Judah's death in 217 C.E. a new group of scholars emerged, the *Amoraim,* speakers or interpreters of the Mishnah. They continued Rabbi Judah's work, adding more oral commentary to his framework, but the Amoraim also took on another task. They translated the words of Torah readings from Hebrew into Aramaic, which was the popular language of the time in Palestine. They embellished their translation to make it more understandable and accessible to listeners.

Two Centers of Study Produce Two Talmuds

After Rabbi Judah's death, the center of Jewish culture and scholarship began to shift from Palestine to Babylon. Each location developed its own traditions and styles of Mishnah, attracting bright students and prospective scholars into their respective schools. New academies were established in Babylon. The most important, Sura, established in the third century, lasted for more than 700 years under the auspices of Rabbi Abba Bar Aivu, aka Abba the Tall One, also known simply as Rav.

It's sometimes difficult for contemporary people to understand the fervor and passion that these ancient scholars had for learning and study. Their goal was not money, but wealth of knowledge. They also vied for audiences, competing through scholarship and piety rather than through material possessions.

Palestinian and Babylonian academies complemented each other from the third through the sixth centuries, as scholars traveled back and forth, sharing ideas and exchanging concepts. In the fourth century, Palestinian Jews were caught in the middle of wars among Roman officials after the fall of the last Severan ruler. This unstable climate once again led to religious and political persecution.

Jews emigrated in large numbers to Babylon, while others moved to the European continent. The established academies suffered as students left. Scholars hurried to finish writing their versions of the Talmud, and the result was two Talmuds: the Babylonian Talmud and the Palestinian Talmud, each reflecting the divergent lives of Jews in their region.

The Babylonian Talmud contained many more legends and parables—*Agada*—than its Palestinian counterpart. Palestinian Jews had a stronger interest in these tales, which were ingrained in their day-to-day storytelling life, so they didn't think it necessary to write them down. Eventually, these Agada were transcribed and constituted a body of work known as *Midrash*. These remain among the most dramatic and touching stories of all religious works. Many of these stories became the basis of parables in other religions that followed. Scores of stories told about Jesus in the Christian Bible were based on Midrash.

The biggest difference between the two Talmuds is their length and scope. Palestinian scholars were cut short in their efforts by political turmoil, so their Talmud was shorter and the editing not as precise. Also, the Babylonian Talmud continued to grow over the next centuries, while the Palestinian version did not. When people refer to the Talmud today, they generally mean the Babylonian Talmud.

By the eleventh century, the Jewish center in Babylon had fallen on hard times, while their counterparts in Spain, Portugal, North Africa, Italy, France, and Germany were flourishing. Because of their proximity to Palestine, the Ashkenazi Jews in Europe looked to the Palestinian Talmud for guidance. The Sephardic Jews in Spain, Portugal, and North Africa studied the Babylonian work.

No matter where they lived, scholars asked questions and stimulated discussion through the practice of *responsa,* which continues today. Responsa are answers to questions asked of rabbis about how the Talmud would interpret an issue. These responsa could pertain to Halakah, individual statutes of law, or be about some religious or cultural matter.

The Talmud Spreads

These new centers of Jewish life produced their own scholars, who began commenting on the Talmud. One was Rabbi Solomon bar Isaac, also known as Rashi, who lived in eleventh-century France. His style differed from that of all the other scholars; he wrote in Hebrew but also mixed in French, German, and other foreign words. By not restricting himself to one language, he was able to find the exact words he needed to keep his comments sharply focused. Rashi was able to comment on the entire Babylonian Talmud and was the first to draw a portrait of Jewish life in the Middle Ages. His work is studied by all Talmudic students today.

Another great commentator was Rabbi Moses Ben Maimon, known to most of us as Maimonides (1135–1204). Born in Spain, Maimonides fled religious persecution and settled in Egypt, where he did most of his work. His greatest accomplishment, the *Mishneh Torah,* took him 10 years to write and the rest of his life to revise. The *Mishneh Torah* comprises all of Jewish law. The original Mishnah referred primarily to the activity of Jews living in Israel, but Maimonides recognized that those outside the holy land needed guidance as well. He interpreted and applied the law to Jews living outside of Israel.

Maimonides distinguished himself by opening his work with a section on philosophy derived mainly from Aristotle's ideas and thoughts. While most other Talmudic commentors eschewed secular Greek philosophy, Maimonides embraced it.

Talmud Censorship

As early as the eighth century, the Catholic Church attempted to stop study of the Talmud. In 1190, the works of Maimonides were burned in Egypt, and during the ensuing years various Church officials, including Pope Gregory IX in 1240 and Pope Clement IV in 1264, ordered Talmuds to be burned, buried, or censored. Their rationale was that the Talmud so tightly bound Jews together that it prevented their conversion to Christianity. Various modern regimes, including that of Russia in the early 1920s, attempted to change Talmudic wording that they didn't like and banned the printing of all Talmuds. Germany's Third Reich destroyed Talmuds in wholesale fashion.

Today, only a few of the original Talmuds that were written in the early academies exist.

Resurgence of Interest in the Talmud

In recent years, there has been a resurgence of interest in the Talmud among Jews and non-Jews mainly because of one scholar's work.

Rabbi Adin Steinsaltz, an Israeli rabbi who holds degrees in mathematics and chemistry, has changed the face of the Talmud. More than anyone in modern times (*Time* magazine called him "a once in a millennium scholar"), he has made the Talmud accessible to millions of people who lack Hebrew language skills.

The Talmud was written in Aramaic and Hebrew without the vowel signs underneath letters that are used in modern Hebrew. The Talmud contained no punctuation marks, so knowing where to begin or end a sentence was a task in itself. Steinsaltz translated the Talmud into modern Hebrew, with punctuation and vowel signs, so anyone who reads the language can now read the work.

Steinsaltz spread out the densely packed text on Talmud pages, so arguments are easier to follow. Steinsaltz also added his own translations of difficult or tricky words into modern Hebrew with his own commentary.

Many ultra-orthodox Jews shunned his efforts, believing that the Talmud should not be altered and that, by making it easier to study, its cachet might be lost. The general public seemed to think otherwise. More than a million copies of Steinsaltz's version in Hebrew have been sold in Israel since it was published in 1990. When the first volumes were translated into English and published in the United States, it sold more than a half-million copies in less than a year.

Many of these readers have discovered the Talmud's sage business advice, which has endured for centuries.

UNLOCKING THE TALMUD'S STRUCTURE

The Talmud contains *orders, tractates,* and *chapters.* There are 6 orders, 63 tractates, and 517 chapters. The sequence of the Talmud is similar to that of the Mishnah.

The first order is *Zeraim,* or the "Seeds," and is devoted to the subjects of agriculture and raising cattle. It discusses such issues as tithing, giving portions of fields to charity, tree grafting, animal husbandry, leaving sections of fields fallow, and the proper way to eat food. This order concerns itself mainly with the practical matters surrounding agriculture, but ethical questions and issues are paramount.

The second order is *Seder Moet,* or "Holidays," and is sometimes labeled "Time." It includes a discussion of the Sabbath, the calendar, and holy days.

The third order is *Nashim,* or "Women," and deals with the relationship between men and women and their obligations to each other. It focuses on marriage, divorce, adultery, vows, and other marital issues.

The fourth order is *Nezikin,* usually translated as "Damages," and deals with laws governing civil and criminal actions. This order is quoted most often in this book, as it contains details on business ethics and laws of commerce. Two of its ten tractates are extremely rich in business-related information: *Bava Metzia* ("Middle Gate") discusses disputes over property, loans, business transactions, sales, hiring and firing employees, and contracting with outside workers. *Bava Batra* ("Last Gate") explains the laws of partnerships, contracts, legal documents, deeds, and other business activities.

Another vital tractate is *Avot,* or "Fathers." This is often broken out into a separate text called *Ethics of the Fathers* or *Sayings of the Fathers,* and it contains some of the richest discussions about ethical obligations.

The fifth order is *Kodashim,* or "Holiness." As its name implies, this order discusses the laws of sacrifices and the dietary laws.

The sixth and last order, *Taharot,* or "Purity," is concerned with cleanliness and keeping healthy.

There is a group of so-called Minor Tractates with subjects that don't seem to fit anywhere else. Some are as long as 10 pages, while others are only a few sentences in length.

A WHO'S WHO OF TALMUDIC RABBIS

We know little about the ancient sages except for their commentary and what others have said about them in the Talmud. Following are introductions to some of the more well-known Talmudic commentators.

Rabbi Akiva (c. 40–135 C.E.)

Rabbi Akiva Ben Josef, considered one of the great Jewish scholars, didn't learn to read or write until he was 40 years old. His life was a tale of conflict between his love for a woman and his love of Torah study.

Akiva worked as a shepherd for one of Jerusalem's richest men, Kalba Savua. Despite his lack of education and abject poverty, Akiva attracted the attention of Kalba's beautiful daughter Rachel. When Rachel looked at Akiva, she didn't see a poor, illiterate shepherd, she saw an intensely pious and righteous man. She married him on the condition that he learn to study Torah. He agreed, and they married in a secret ceremony.

When her father discovered their secret marriage, he threw them out of the house. The couple was so poor that while he was learning to read and write, Akiva collected sticks and branches to make a living. Half he would sell and the other half he would burn so that he could study by the light of the fire and heat their hovel. Rachel sold locks of her hair to allow Akiva to study.

Rachel gave Akiva permission to travel to the city of Lod to study Talmud. He returned 12 years later and heard a man asking his wife, "How long will you continue to be a widow while your husband is alive?" Without knowing that Akiva was overhearing, she replied, "If he could listen to my voice, I would tell him to continue his studies for another twelve years." Although Akiva loved his wife, he also loved Torah study. Without revealing himself to his wife, he returned to Lod.

He came home 12 years later, accompanied by 24,000 disciples. As he approached Rachel, she tripped. As one of his students was about to brush her aside Akiva shouted, "Don't touch her! What is mine and what is yours all belongs to her."

To the modern ear this may sound patronizing, but in those days it was unheard of for a famous man to admit, especially in front of devoted disciples, that a woman was responsible for his success.

Hearing that a famous scholar was coming to town, Rachel's father prepared to meet him. He didn't know that the scholar was his disowned son-in-law. When Akiva revealed who he was, Savua admitted his mistake and gave the couple half of his fortune. Akiva and Rachel thus became rich, and Akiva kept a promise he had made many years before. "If I had the means," Akiva had told Rachel when they first married, "I would buy you a Jerusalem of Gold." (This was an ornament featuring a picture of the city.) When he became rich, Akiva bought that ornament for Rachel, only to be admonished by his students for being ostentatious. Akiva replied, "She suffered a lot of pain with me for Torah."

Once, Akiva was questioned by a disciple, "Rabbi, who is rich?" He answered, "One who has the love of a woman."

Akiva suffered one last time for his beliefs when the Roman government arrested him for teaching Torah to assembled masses and tortured him to death.

Rabbi Ashi (352–427)

Rabbi Ashi was head of the Sura Academy for 56 years, and was most well known for his role with his pupil and colleague Ravina in assembling and arranging the Babylonian Talmud. He was a wealthy and serious man who slept inside a synagogue during its reconstruction to make sure the job was done to his specifications.

Rabbi Elazar ben Azaryah

Elazar was asked to be a teacher when he was only 18 years old. Fearing that students and other scholars would not respect his young age, he prayed for a miracle. Overnight, his hair turned gray and his new appearance commanded respect. He is noted for his comment: "Where there is no money, there is no learning." He also was remembered for saying that on the Day of Atonement, Yom Kippur, asking God for forgiveness is not as important as asking other people for their forgiveness.

Hillel

Hillel Hazaken, one of the most famous Tannaim, or commentators, on the Mishnah, endured poverty to study Torah. One time he didn't have the small coin that he usually gave the guard at the school, so he climbed to the roof and listened through a small window. It was very cold and snow began falling. In the morning, the teachers Schemata and Avalon noticed the room's darkness and thought it was overcast. They looked up and saw a person slumped over the window. When they reached the roof, they found Hillel, partially frozen. They brought him inside and nursed him back to health. The entry fee was abolished after this incident.

Hillel was known as the innovator behind *prosbul,* a system that ensured the availability of loans to poor people. He is remembered for his response to the heathen who wanted to convert to Judaism on the condition that Hillel teach him the entire Torah while standing on one foot. Hillel agreed and said, "What is hateful to you, do not do to anyone else. This is the whole of Torah; the rest is commentary." Hillel's most famous saying is: "If I am not for myself, then who will be for me? And if I am only for myself, then what am I? And if not now, when?"

Hillel often interpreted scripture more liberally and humanistically than his more hard-line contemporaries, especially Shammai. Scholars suggest that at an early age Jesus became a rabbi in the House of Hillel. He saw himself as a reformer, trying to work within the Jewish tradition to improve it, but later moving further away from accepted dogma with many of his ideas coming from his broad-minded teacher Hillel. The Hillel organization, a network of Jewish college student groups, bears his name.

Rabbi Huna

Rabbi Huna headed the yeshiva of Sura for more than 40 years. When he taught, he was surrounded by 13 *amoraim,* who would deliver and elaborate on his lectures. He had more than 800 students.

On Sabbath eve, Huna would send a messenger to the marketplace to buy fruits and vegetables and throw what he didn't use into the river so it couldn't be taken from the trash and sold the following week. He didn't distribute the unused food to the poor for fear that they would rely on it and not purchase their own food. When asked why he purchased more food than he needed, he replied that the farmers might not grow adequate supplies if they thought there would be leftovers. The price would rise and the poor would suffer.

Rabbi Yohannan ben Zakkai

Yohannan was a student of Hillel. It's said that he lived for 120 years, dividing his life into three periods: He worked in business for 40 years, studied for 40 years, and taught for 40 years.

He lived in Jerusalem during a time of harsh Roman reign, and he was imprisoned. He was placed in a dark cell, where he was harassed by guards who periodically asked him what time it was. If he answered wrong, he would be tortured. Yohannan was able to give the guards the correct time because he had studied Mishnah chapters day and night, and he knew how long it took for each one.

Rabbi Meir

Rabbi Meir was called "the illuminator" because he enlightened scholars in Jewish law. Meir delivered sermons every Friday evening, and one time the lecture was so long that a woman who attended came home very late. Her angry husband questioned her whereabouts—it was considered inadvisable for a woman to be out alone at night—and she said that she had been listening to a lecture. The husband demanded that she not go back until she spit in the face of the lecturer. Meir heard about this incident and pretended that he needed someone to spit in his eye to dislodge a foreign object. The woman reluctantly agreed to do so, not once but seven times as Meir requested. Meir said, "Tell your husband that he only told you to spit once, but you spit seven times." When questioned by his students about this shame on a

Torah scholar, Meir noted that there is no higher duty to God than to make peace between a husband and a wife.

One of Meir's most poignant statements is this: "When a person enters the world, his hands are clenched as if to say 'the whole world is mine.' When a person leaves the world, his hands are open."

Maimonides (1135–1204)

Rabbi Moses Ben Maimon, also known as the RaMBaM, was born in Spain. He fled religious persecution and settled in Egypt, where he did most of his work in the twelfth century. His greatest works are the *Mishneh Torah* ("the second law") and *The Guide of the Perplexed*, in which he tried to reconcile Aristotle's theories with those of Jewish theology. This helped to introduce Aristotle to the Christian philosophers of the Middle Ages. He was a physician and wrote medical works as well.

Rashi (1040–1105)

Rabbi Solomon bar Isaac, or Rashi, lived in eleventh-century France and wrote in Hebrew but mixed in French, German, and other languages to keep his comments sharply focused. Rashi was able to comment on the entire Babylonian Talmud, and his work is considered by many to be the best commentary ever written. Almost every edition of the Talmud printed since the invention of the printing press includes Rashi's commentary.

Rav Papa

Rav Papa was head of an academy near Sura. Although born poor, he became expert at brewing dates and became wealthy. He never attributed his wealth to his business acumen, but said it was because his wife was descended from a high priest, or *Kohane*. His comments are often the last quoted in discussions, and he took on the role of conciliator among disputing rabbis. It is said that he was so impressed by the scholarship of one of his students that he kissed the neophyte's hand and offered his daughter in marriage. Rav Papa was a strong advocate for self-reliance, advising people to sow corn for their own use so they wouldn't have to be dependent on anyone else and to acquire land.

Ravina

Ravina is best remembered for his compiling of the Babylonian Talmud with his teacher Rabbi Ashi. There is little else known about him.

BIBLIOGRAPHY

Books

Amsel, Nachum. *The Jewish Encyclopedia of Moral and Ethical Issues.* Northvale, NJ: Jason Aronson, Inc., 1996.

Bialik, Hayim Nahman, and Yehoshua Hana Ravnitzky, eds. *The Book of Legends, Sefer Ha-Aggadah: Legends from the Talmud and Midrash.* New York: Schocken Books, 1992.

Bianco, Anthony. *The Reichmanns: Family, Faith, Fortune, and the Empire of Olympia & York.* New York: Vintage Books USA, 1998.

Blech, Benjamin (Rabbi). *The Complete Idiot's Guide to Jewish History and Culture.* New York: Alpha Books, 1999.

Bokser, Ben Zion, trans. *The Talmud: Selected Writings.* New York: Paulist Press, 1989.

Bonder, Nilton. *The Kabbalah of Money.* Boston: Shambala, 1996.

Cohen, Abraham. *Everyman's Talmud: The Major Teachings of the Rabbinic Sages.* New York: Schocken Books, 1949.

Evans, Frank C., and David M. Bishop. *Valuation for M&A: Building Value in Private Companies.* New York: John Wiley & Sons, 2001.

Finkel, Avraham Yaakov. *The Great Torah Commentators.* Northvale, NJ: Jason Aronson, Inc., 1996.

Frieman, Shulamis. *Who's Who in the Talmud.* Northvale, NJ: Jason Aronson, Inc., 1995.

Goldin, Barbara Diamond. *The Family Book of Midrash: 52 Jewish Stories from the Sages.* Northvale, NJ: Jason Aronson, Inc., 1990.

Hertz, Joseph H. *Pirke Avot (Sayings of the Fathers).* West Orange, NJ: Behrman House, Inc., 1945.

Isaacs, Ronald H. *Words for the Soul: Jewish Wisdom for Life's Journey.* Northvale, NJ: Jason Aronson, Inc., 1996.

Jung, Leo. *Business Ethics in Jewish Law* (with a concluding section, "Jewish Ethics in Contemporary Society," by Aaron Levine). New York: Hebrew Publishing Company, 1987.

Levine, Aaron. *Economics & Jewish Law.* Hoboken, NJ: KTAV Publishing House, Inc., and Yeshiva University Press, 1987.

Levine, Aaron. *Economic Public Policy and Jewish Law.* Hoboken, NJ: KTAV Publishing House, Inc., 1993.

Levine, Aaron. *Free Enterprise and Jewish Law.* New York: KTAV Publishing House, Inc., and Yeshiva University Press, 1980.

Neusner, Jacob. *The Economics of the Mishnah.* Chicago: University of Chicago Press, 1990.

Neusner, Jacob. *Invitation to the Talmud.* San Francisco: Harper San Francisco, 1984.

Newman, Louis I., ed., and Samuel Spitz, collab. *The Talmudic Anthology.* West Orange, NJ: Behrman House, Inc., 1945.

Stack, H. L., and G. Stemberger. *Introduction to the Talmud and Midrash.* Minneapolis: Fortress Press, 1992.

Steinsaltz, Adin. *The Essential Talmud.* New York: HarperCollins, 1976.

Steinsaltz, Adin. *The Talmud: The Steinsaltz Edition.* New York: Random House, 1989–1997.

Tamari, Meir. *The Challenge of Wealth.* Northvale, NJ: Jason Aronson, Inc., 1995.

Tamari, Meir. *In the Marketplace: Jewish Business Ethics.* Southfield, MI: Targum Press, Inc., 1991.

Telushkin, Joseph. *Jewish Wisdom*. New York: William Morrow and Company, Inc., 1994.

Wagschal, S. *Torah Guide for the Businessman*. Jerusalem–New York: Feldheim Publishers, 1990.

Wolpe, David J. *Why Be Jewish?* New York: Henry Holt, 1995.

CD-ROMs

The Soncino Talmud. Chicago: Davka Corporation, 1991–1995.

Dissertations

Zipperstein, Edward. "Business Ethics in Jewish Law" (doctoral diss., Hebrew Union College–Jewish Institute of Religion), California, 1981.

Periodicals and News Services

Anderson, Sarah, "Wal-Mart's War on Main Street," *The Progressive* 58 (November 1, 1994): 19–21.

Atkinson, Marcia, "Build Learning into Work," *HR Magazine* 39 (September 1, 1994): 60–63.

Aumann, Robert J., and Michael Maschler, "Game Theoretic Analysis of a Bankruptcy Problem from the Talmud," *Journal of Economic Theory* (Jerusalem) 36 (1985): 195–213.

Bencivenga, Dominic, "Learning Organizations Evolve in New Directions," *HR Magazine* 40 (October 1, 1995): 69–73.

Bush, Lawrence, and Jeffrey Dekro, "Jews, Money and Social Responsibility," *Tikkun* 8, no. 5 (September-October 1993): 33–37.

Caudron, Shari, "Forget Image; It's Your Reputation That Matters," *Industry Week* 246, no. 3 (February 3, 1997): 13–15.

Coffman, Richard B., "Some Economic Implications of Talmudic Business Ethics," *Akron Business and Economic Review* (Spring 1982): 24–27.

Cohen, Debra Nussbaum, "New Forms of Jewish Charity Evolving Based on Religious, Social Values," Jewish Telegraphic Agency 29 September 1993.

Corcoran, Elizabeth, "A Flaw Chips Away at Intel's Shiny Image," *Washington Post,* 2 December 1994, A1.

Ettore, Barbara, "The Care and Feeding of a Corporate Reputation," *Management Review* 85, no. 6 (June 1996): 39–42.

Friedman, Hershey H., "Ancient Marketing Practices: The View from Talmudic Times," *Journal of Public Policy & Marketing* 3 (1984): 194–204.

Friedman, Hershey H., "Ethical Behavior in Business: A Hierarchical Approach from the Talmud," *Journal of Business Ethics* 4 (1985): 117–129.

Friedman, Hershey H., "Talmudic Business Ethics: An Historical Perspective," *Akron Business and Economic Review* (Winter 1980): 45–49.

Gibbs, Nancy R., "Begging: To Give or Not to Give," *Time* (September 5, 1988).

Ginsburg, Steven, "More Companies Now Come with a Campus," *Washington Post* 14 September 1997, H-4.

Hakohen, Josef Ben-Schlomo, "Talmudic Teachings on Pollution and Love of Land, Hassidic Ecology," *Jerusalem Post* 29 April 1990.

Hauptman, Judith, "Judaism and a Just Economy," *Tikkun* 9, no. 1: 55–57.

Jones, Glenda Shasho, "Solving the Identity Crisis: Branding Helps Direct Mailers and Catalogers Gain Consumer Trust and Confidence," *Direct* 9, no. 5 (April 1997): 88–89.

Jossi, Frank, "Branding Breaks New Ground," *Potentials in Marketing* 29, no. 11 (November 1996): 13–16.

Kleiman, Ephraim, "Just Price in Talmudic Literature," *History of Political Economy* 19, no. 1 (1987): 23–45.

Kleiman, Ephraim, "Opportunity Cost, Human Capital and Some Related Economic Concepts in Talmudic Literature," *History of Political Economy* 19, no. 2 (1987): 261–287.

Konvitz, Milton R., "Natural Law and Judaism: The Case of Maimonides," *Judaism* 45, no. 1 (Winter 1996).

Lehman-Wilzig, Sam, "Oppositionism in the Jewish Heritage," *Judaism* 40 (January 1, 1991): 16.

Levine, Aaron, "Opportunity Cost as Treated in Talmudic Literature," *Tradition* 15, no. 1-2 (Spring-Summer 1975): 153–172.

Makower, Joel, ed., *The Green Business Letter* (May 1994, June 1996).

McCarthy, Joseph L., "Through the Needle's Eye: The Spiritual CEO," *Chief Executive* (January/February 1996).

Modeland, Vern, "Juiceless Baby Juice Leads to Full-Length Justice," *FDA Consumer* 22 (June 1, 1988): 14(4).

Nichols, Don, "The Pause That Refreshes: More Restaurant Companies Are Using Sabbaticals to Help Managers Recharge and Refocus," *Restaurant Business* 95, no. 2, (January 20, 1996): 26–28.

Ohrenstein, Roman A., "Business Cycle Analysis in Talmudic Literature," *International Journal of Social Economics* 20, no. 1: 41–50.

Ohrenstein, Roman A., "Value Analysis in Talmudic Literature in the Light of Modern Economics," *International Journal of Social Economics* 13, no. 3: 34–52.

Ohrenstein, Roman A., and Barry Gordon, "Some Aspects of Human Capital in Talmudic Literature," *International Journal of Social Economics* 14, no. 3/4/5: 185–190.

Pava, Moses L., "The Talmudic Concept of Beyond the Letter of the Law: Relevance to Business Social Responsibility," *Journal of Business Ethics* 14, no. 9 (September 1996).

Rigby, Darrell, "Look Before You Layoff," *Harvard Business Review* (March 2002).

Romano, Catherine, "Time Out: Offering Employees Sabbaticals and Leaves of Absence," *Management Review* 84, no. 1 (January 1995): 26–29.

Rosenblatt, Gary, "Between the Lines: Strengthening Jewish Outreach," *The Jewish Week* (August 16, 1996).

Rosenstein, Pinchas, "Baring's Bank—Self-Regulation, A Jewish Perspective," Center for Business Ethics newsletter, Jerusalem College of Technology, Summer 1994.

Schnall, David J., "Exploratory Notes on Employee Productivity and Accountability and Classic Jewish Sources," *Journal of Business Ethics* 12, no. 6 (June 1993).

Scott, Janny, "In the Urban Maelstrom, the Faithful Persevere," *New York Times* 5 March 1995, late edition, sec. 1, p. 1.

Sheley, Elizabeth, "Why Give Employees Sabbaticals?," *HR Magazine* 41, no. 3 (March 1996): 58–65.

Tamari, Meir, "Competition: Justice and Mercy," Center for Business Ethics newsletter, Jerusalem College of Technology, vol. 2, no. 4.

Tellis, Gerard, and Peter Golder, "First to Market, First to Fail? Real Causes of Enduring Market Leadership," *Sloan Management Review* 37, no. 2 (Winter 1996): 65–75.

Walsh, Sharon, "Captains Courteous; Era of the Brutal Boss May be Giving Way to a New Sensitivity at the Top," *Washington Post* 31 August 1997, H-1.

Zoll, Daniel, "U.S. Business: Retailer Goes Abroad as Discontent Brews at Home," Inter Press Service English News Wire, 22 March 1997.

Speeches

Cohen, Gerson, "The Unwritten Law of Business in the Talmud." speech delivered at first session, Seminar on Talmudic Ethics, Jewish Theological Seminary, New York, October 24, 1958.

Web Sites

American Society for Training and Development, www.astd.org

Ohr Somayach International, www.ohr.org

Page of Talmud, www.ucalgary.ca/~elsegal/TalmudPage.html

Project Genesis, www.torah.org/learning/

Sprawl-Busters, www.sprawl-busters.com

INDEX